Turbine Ste

of the British Isles

Nick Robins

This book is dedicated to the memory of my father, George, whose enthusiasm for the sea kindled my own interest in shipping.

Although employed as a Chartered Geologist, Nick Robins maintains a long standing passion for the sea and its shipping. Interest has concentrated on British and Irish flag short-sea routes as well as the deep sea liner services operated under the Red Ensign. A keen shipping photographer, he began by photographing ships on the Manchester Ship Canal in 1960, but quickly progressed to include all the major British and Irish passenger carriers that have seen service since the mid-1960s. His photographs have appeared in numerous magazines and books. Nick Robins is also the author of a number of articles in *Sea Breezes* and other journals, and of several books, not least *The Evolution of the British Ferry* and *The British Excursion Ship*. He is married with four children.

6 5 4 3 2 1

Designed by Colourpoint Books, Newtownards
Cover design: Barry Craig at Colourpoint
Printed by W&G Baird Ltd

ISBN 1 898392 38 2

Colourpoint Books
Unit D5, Ards Business Centre
Jubilee Road
NEWTOWNARDS
County Down
Northern Ireland
BT23 4YH
Tel: (028 91) 820505
Fax: (028 91) 821900
E-mail: Info@colourpoint.co.uk
Web-site: www.colourpoint.co.uk

Front cover: *Queen Mary* currently in static use alongside the Embankment, London.
Nick Robins

Title page: *Caledonian Princess* (1961) at Fishguard.
Nick Robins

Rear cover: *Duke of Lancaster* on a daylight sailing from Heysham to Belfast in August 1969.
Ian Harmsworth

Contents

List of Tables

List of Figures

Introduction

The story of the British turbine-driven cross-channel steamer is one of both engineering innovation and nostalgia for an era of travel now past. Sir Charles Parsons, the Parsons Marine Steam Turbine Company and shipbuilders such as William Denny of Dumbarton are the key elements, but the stars are the actual steamers. The routine of successful and regular service, the triumphs and tragedies, and the men and women who served on the ships provide a fascinating and important part of our maritime history in the Twentieth Century.

The book records all the British flag turbine steamers from the *King Edward* of 1901 to the *Ben-my-Chree* of 1966. It records the dramatic rise in numbers of this distinctive form of coastal ship during the early Twentieth Century, as well as the equally rapid fall from popularity sixty years later, when faced with ever rising fuel costs and increasingly efficient diesel engines. A total of 36 direct drive triple screw steamers were built between 1901 and 1912, although three excursion steamers were also built for use on the Clyde between 1930 and 1933; 77 single reduction geared steamers were built between 1911 and 1951; and 15 double reduction geared steamers were commissioned after World War II.

Thanks are due to my friends: Richard Danielson, Ian Harmsworth, Malcolm McRonald, Kevin Le Scelleur, John Shepherd and Mike Walker, to the P&O Steam Navigation Company and to FotoFlite for permission to reproduce photographic material. I am particularly grateful to Malcolm McRonald and my late father George Robins for critically reviewing the manuscript.

Crowmarsh, Oxfordshire

THE PARSONS' LEGACY

In 1894 a new form of marine motive power was realised when Charles Parsons, later Sir Charles Parsons, invented his turbine engine. Parsons demonstrated his new engine with the steam turbine experimental torpedo boat, the *Turbinia.* This 45 ton steel launch rudely charged at 34 knots through the lines of the 1897 British Naval Review at Spithead, which was celebrating Queen Victoria's Diamond Jubilee. The boat had been built by Parsons specifically to demonstrate his new form of power at this prestigious international event. The vessel had three separate turbine units driving three shafts and propellers.

Sir Charles had developed his prototype engine almost single handed. He was soon to see the reward – the Admiralty immediately ordered two turbine driven torpedo-destroyers. By 1905 the epoch-making turbine driven battleship *Dreadnought* had been launched at Portsmouth. Parsons realised that expansion of steam over successive turbines of increasing size would moderate the speed of the steam on the blades and provide much improved efficiency; the *Dreadnought* had four shafts. The two wing shafts had one high pressure ahead and one high pressure astern turbine, and the amidships shafts each had one low pressure ahead and one low pressure astern turbine. Each turbine had 39,600 blades. On trials the ship was only able to reach her design speed of 22 knots for brief occasions but, later on in her career (when the engineering crew were more familiar with her complex machinery), she was able to attain the required speed without difficulty. The cost of this new type of capital ship, was £1,797,497, a considerable proportion of the 1905/6 defence budget.

The first transatlantic liners to be commissioned with turbine drive were the 15,000 ton Allan Line sisters *Victorian* and *Virginian.* Their machinery could produce 11,000 kilowatts. In 1905, the Cunard Line commissioned the sisters *Carmania* and *Caronia*, identical twins save for their machinery. The *Carmania* was equipped with Parsons turbines and three shafts, with two low pressure turbines on the wing shafts and one high pressure turbine on the central shaft. The *Caronia* had conventional steam reciprocating engines. Under similar operating conditions the turbine ship could attain over 20 knots, whereas the piston engined ship could only get up to 19 knots.

Before long, the 32,000 ton liner *Mauretania* was crossing the Atlantic at 25 knots, (gaining her the Blue Riband which she retained for over twenty years), using four turbines which provided over 52,000 kilowatts shaft power to drive four high-speed propellers. The high pressure turbines drove the wing propellers and the low pressure turbines the inner propellers. The propellers were initially three-bladed and were 3.6 m in diameter, the outer pair being inward turning and the inner pair outward turning. The turbines themselves were massive: the high pressure turbine rotors were 2.5 m in diameter and weighed 72 tons each while the low pressure turbines were 3.6 m in diameter, 14.6 m long and weighed 130 tons each. The choice of machinery had been decided by a government commission comprising representatives of John Brown, Swan Hunter, William Denny, the Wallsend Slipway & Engineering Company, Lloyds, the Admiralty and, of course, Parsons himself (there was an outstanding soft Government loan with Cunard at the time of £2.5 million).

There were also several other important developments taking place. For example, the transmission of the greater power that the turbines provided was only possible with the introduction of the Highbury and Mitchell rocking pad bearing in 1905. In due course, the geared turbine engine allowed the high speed turbine, at several thousand revolutions per minute, to drive a propeller at an efficient rate of 90 to 300 revolutions per minute. Not only was the simplicity of the engine advantageous to shipowners of the day, but so too was the favourable power to weight ratio compared with the conventional steam reciprocating engine.

By 1938 the mighty Cunarder *Queen Elizabeth* could attain speeds over 30 knots from turbine power of 135,000 kilowatts. The last of the British-flagged turbine driven liners (turbo-electric drive) was the P&O cruise liner *Canberra* which was only retired in 1997. The turbo-electric principal lives on, however, as all electricity generating power stations, whether fired by coal or nuclear fuel, generate steam to drive turbines which turn the generators - the latter often referred to as the conventional side in a nuclear station.

The basic turbine is a fixed outer cylinder from which numerous vanes project - this is the stator. A coaxial shaft within the cylinder also carries numerous vanes, and steam directed onto the blades of the stator is deflected onto the corresponding blades of the shaft or rotor, and causes it to revolve. The steam can be expanded through up to four turbines at decreasing pressure before being condensed and returned to the boiler. The condenser extracts the last vestige of energy from the steam by creating a vacuum; and the faster that the turbine operates, the better is the thermal efficiency.

But what of the short sea world? William Denny the shipbuilder at Dumbarton on the Lower Clyde had already a considerable reputation for the design and construction of cross-channel ships. The company foresaw the potential of the turbine and approached Parsons directly. Parsons was keen to cooperate, but it was a day excursion steamer that was to become the testbed of the turbine concept for commercial use. This was the *King Edward*, launched at Dumbarton on 16th May 1901 to the order of the Turbine Steamer Syndicate, and placed under the management of a new company called Turbine Steamers Limited. She was built with the express intention of demonstrating the turbine engine on a commercial scale, and in particular, the potential of this form of motive power for passenger ships. Denny put up most of the capital, providing some £24,200, with Parsons providing a further £8,000 and Williamson the shipowner only £800 as an operational fund.

The *King Edward* had three direct acting turbines built by the Parsons' company at Wallsend, the higher pressure turbine connected to the central propeller and the lower pressure turbines to the wing propellers. The central propeller was 1.4 m in diameter, and the outer pair each had two sets of 1.0 m diameter propellers set one 3 m in front of the other, but these were found to create cavitation at speed and were replaced by single propellers in 1905. Steam was provided at a pressure of 10 bar. The reverse turbines were incorporated in the low pressure casings. This arrangement produced 2,600 kilowatts and gave her a speed of 20.5 knots on trials, with a noticeable absence of vibration. The design speed of the wing propellers was 755 revolutions per minute. The efficiency of the new machinery was illustrated by her ability to steam at 18 knots on one ton of coal for 14.2 kilometres, whereas the contemporary paddle steamer *Duchess of Hamilton*, which was of almost identical dimensions to the *King Edward*, then only managed 13.2 kilometres at 16 knots using the same quantity of fuel.

The gross tonnage of the *King Edward* was only 562. She was of conventional construction, transverse framed throughout with a Main Deck and a Weather Deck. Dining and deck saloons were arranged for the first class passengers aft and for third class passengers forward. The *King Edward* could accommodate 1,966 passengers; her accommodation was very traditional and was designed along the lines of the paddle steamers of the day.

The *King Edward* was placed on a long day excursion route, that of Greenock to Campbeltown, and was an immediate success with the travelling public. So successful was the commercial venture, that a consort, the *Queen Alexandra*, was

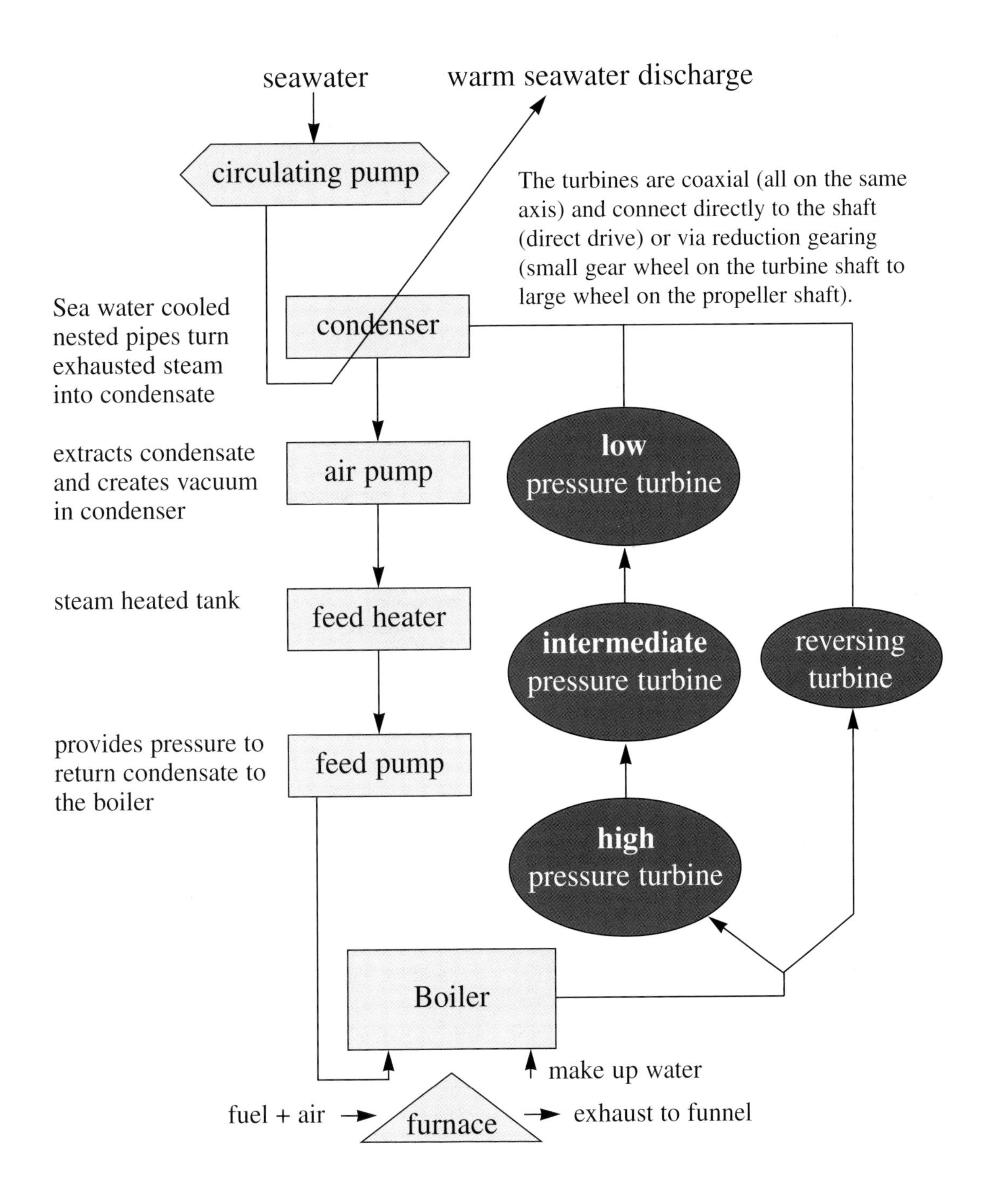

Figure 1.
The marine turbine steam cycle.

The first *Queen Alexandra* (1902) served only nine years on the Clyde before she was gutted by fire.
(Glasgow University)

constructed and commissioned in 1902. This ship was slightly larger than her sister and had a length of 80 m. She was placed on a service which took her to Ardrishaig and later to Inveraray in competition with the established paddler *Lord of the Isles* of 1891. After ten years sharing the route with the turbine ships, Turbine Steamers Limited bought the old paddle steamer and put her onto another service. Sadly, this was brought about by the loss of the *Queen Alexandra* in 1911 by fire whilst alongside at Greenock; she was later renovated and sold to Canadian Pacific Railways for use out of Vancouver. A replacement turbine steamer of the same name was delivered in 1912; she was of almost identical design to the *King Edward*. The new ship was renamed *Saint Columba* in 1936 and was eventually disposed of for scrap in 1958.

Given the immediate success of the two Clyde day-excursion ships, the obvious role of the marine turbine engine for fast passage on shallow draught cross-channel and other ferry services was quickly recognised by the railway companies and others. On the Dover Strait, the last paddle steamer ordered by the South Eastern & Chatham Railway, the *Mabel Grace*, was completed only in 1899. The first turbine steamer, *The Queen*, arrived in 1903, and without any intermediate transition via piston driven screw steamers, a succession of new turbine ships saw all the paddlers off the Dover Strait by 1910.

The Queen was the first cross channel turbine steamer in the world. During 1902 the South Eastern & Chatham Railway was persuaded by Denny to introduce turbine steamers to their prestigious routes. The first ship was offered at a

The first cross-channel turbine steamer in the world, *The Queen* (1903). (National Maritime Museum)

cost of £83,000 with the proviso that if she failed to perform to the required standard, the builders would buy her back. As it was, she set the standard for the next decade. She initially had five screws but the outer pair, which were designed to reduce cavitation on the inner set, were discarded during trials. Her high pressure turbine drove the central screw, and the wing shafts were connected to low pressure turbines, collectively providing 5,600 kilowatts. Two boilers supplied steam at 10 bar. On trials she attained 20.8 knots (13 knots astern) and during her first season maintained an operating speed of 20 knots with ease. Her propeller speed was 800 revolutions per minute.

Four sisters followed between 1905 and 1907: the *Onward, Invicta, Victoria* and *Empress*. These ships all attained trials speeds of between 22.5 and 22.7 knots. The *Onward* was of 1,691 tons gross and could accommodate 1,500 passengers; she was ultimately scrapped in 1946. The *Victoria* survived until 1957, having then spent the greater part of her career on the Irish Sea, whereas the *Invicta* and the *Empress* were both broken up in 1933. The pioneer steamer *The Queen* sadly only survived until 1916, being lost off Folkestone when she was attacked by German destroyers.

Elsewhere, there was a transition period from paddle wheel to steam reciprocating engines coupled to screws, before the turbine engine ships took their place on many of the fast and prestigious services. There were few major routes where turbine ships never operated; one was the Liverpool to Belfast service, which progressed from triple screw steam piston engines all the way to diesel engines with the arrival of the *Ulster Monarch* class in the late 1920s. Another was the Liverpool to Dublin route.

Nevertheless, the clamour for the Parsons' direct-drive turbine engine coupled with William Denny design, was to guarantee both companies a long and lucrative partnership. The first turbine steamer to run on the Irish routes was the Denny-built *Princess Maud*, ordered for the Stranraer to Larne service from Denny's yard with delivery in 1904. She had a gross tonnage of 1,746 and was driven by the normal arrangement of one central high pressure and two wing low pressure turbines. The design was repeated eight years later when the *Princess Victoria* joined her from the same builders.

The first large motor driven cross-channel ship, *Ulster Monarch* (1929) - dawn arrival at Liverpool summer 1966. (author)

In the intervening years the cost of building had risen from £66,100 for the first ship to £70,700 for the second. Both vessels lasted until the early thirties when they were withdrawn and scrapped.

Other builders inevitably joined this success. A notable early turbine steamer was the *Viking* built by Armstrong, Whitworth on the Tyne to the order of the Isle of Man Steam Packet Company at a cost of £83,900. She was 107 m long, by 13 m broad and had a gross tonnage of 1,957. Boiler steam was delivered to the high pressure turbine at 11 bar and the collective power of her three turbines was 7,500 kilowatts. She was easily capable of her design speed of 22 knots and made a Fleetwood to Douglas crossing in 1907 at an average speed of 23.2 knots. John Brown at Clydebank, and Vickers Sons & Maxim at Barrow were two of the first shipbuilders to build their own turbine engines; the *Atalanta* (1906) for the Glasgow & South Western Railway and the *Ben-my-Chree* (1908) for the Isle of Man Steam Packet Company are respective examples.

The next phase in the marine turbine was the development of the single reduction gear. This enabled a more efficient couple between the turbine and the propeller. During 1909, the engine room of a conventional steam reciprocating driven cargo ship with a gross tonnage of 4,300 was stripped out at the Wallsend Turbinia Works and a set of Parsons turbines coupled to single reduction gearing was substituted. Tests showed that the turbine could drive the ship with the same efficiency as the steam reciprocating engine via the reduction gearing and using the existing conventional low speed propeller. This demonstrated that the single reduction gear was viable. Much later in the 1950s, double reduction gearing was introduced to allow even higher and more efficient turbine operating speeds to be achieved.

The propeller speed of the old triple-screw direct-drive turbine ships was about 600 revolutions per minute. Gearing allowed this to be reduced to a more efficient 270 revolutions per minute along

Viking (1905), a ship which was to have an operational career of nearly 50 years. (John Shepherd collection)

with an increased operating speed of the turbine. The latter permitted far greater thermal efficiency to be achieved from the steam supply. By way of comparison, a contemporary diesel driven ferry using variable pitch propellers to control the ship's velocity operates with a constant propeller speed of about 275 revolutions per minute.

Typical of the early single reduction geared turbine era, were the 24 knot cross-channel steamers *Biarritz* and *Maid of Orleans* which were commissioned in 1915 and 1918 respectively. The London & North Western Railway brought out the sisters *Anglia, Cambria, Hibernia* and *Scotia* in 1920 and 1921, each with a capability of 25 knots. Other notable examples include the *Dinard* and *St Briac* and the *Isle of Thanet* in the period 1924/5, but all of these fine ships had a common builder - William Denny of Dumbarton.

In order to demonstrate the role of high pressure steam for the marine turbine, Parsons Marine Steam Turbines along with Yarrow Boilers, William Denny and Turbine Steamers Limited, built and commissioned the *King George V* in 1926. She cost £69,648 of which her engines and naval type boilers came to some £29,000. Like the first commercial turbine steamer, the *King Edward*, she was placed in service as a Clyde excursion steamer. Steam was supplied from two Yarrow boilers at an exceptionally high temperature of 400°C with an operating pressure of 38 bar. This was fed to the port unit which was quadruple expansion, and exhausted to the central and starboard units which were triple expansion. The turbines were coupled to twin propellers by reduction gearing. With her engines running at 582 revolutions per minute she reached 20.8 knots on trials.

At the end of the 1927 season tragedy struck when a boiler tube burst, blowing off the furnace doors and killing two men. The boilers were replaced in 1929 with two Babcock and Wilcox boilers operating at more conventional pressures. These were again replaced in 1936 when the operating pressure was further reduced to 16 bar and the extra high pressure turbine removed. This brought her operating speed down to an economical 16 knots, her demonstration role now over. This did not prevent her from carrying out royal duties when the King, accompanied by Queen

Mary, was carried on the upper Clyde in July 1931. The ship originally had a gross tonnage of 789 and incorporated a fully enclosed lounge forward, a novel feature on Clyde steamers. She could accommodate 1,250 passengers. After a long and successful career as a Clyde excursion steamer and latterly as the Oban day-steamer for David MacBrayne, she adopted a static role at Cardiff where she was later gutted by fire in 1981.

Although coal had always been the preferred fuel, oil, which was far more convenient to use, secured favour during the miners strike of 1926. Use of oil fuel also allowed exhaust fumes to be drawn to a single funnel, dispensing with the need for two funnels and considerably altering the profile of the fast ferry and excursion ships thereafter. Many coal burners were subsequently converted for oil burning. The depressed years of the 1930s and the years of hardship and utility that followed lessened the need for fast ferry services, and ships were increasingly designed for speeds below 20 knots. The role of the turbine steamer in British waters is nevertheless graphically illustrated in Figure 2, which shows the sharp uptake of the direct-drive turbine concept for fast shallow draught shipping and the success of the geared turbine on short sea routes.

In the late 1940s and early 1950s a new higher pressure turbine design was being developed jointly by Parsons' and the Marine Engineers Turbine Research and Development Association (Pametrada). Coupled with double reduction gearing rather than just single gearing, the new Pametrada design enabled faster, and more efficient turbine speeds to be achieved, along with slower shaft speeds.

In the 1950s and 1960s the whole concept of ferry travel underwent considerable upheaval. No longer was the ferry seen as a seaborne extension of the land based railway routes, but as a means of crossing to Ireland and the Continent with a car. The steam turbine engine was well able to cope with the demands of the marine architect for the vehicle ferry, and did so in Britain to a late stage because of the abject conservatism of the chief technical officer in the Shipping & International Services Division within British Rail. The overall reason for the decline in popularity of the turbine was the vastly improved efficiency of the modern internal combustion engine coupled with ever

Avalon (1963), the ultimate although not the last turbine steamer, was built at a cost of £2 million. (author)

rising fuel costs.

The last steam turbine ferries designed for the British Railways Board were the *Avalon*, a conventional passenger and cargo ferry later converted to a drive-on ferry, and the stern loading ferries *Holyhead Ferry I* and the *Dover*, the latter delivered in 1965. The *Avalon* had twin sets of Pametrada turbines which produced 1,100 kilowatts, to maintain a day-time service speed of 21 knots between Harwich and the Hook of Holland; the night-time service was scheduled to take rather longer. The equally conservative outlook of the then board of the Isle of Man Steam Packet Company also clung to the old technology, and the *Manx Maid* and *Ben-my-Chree*, both side-loading steam turbine driven car ferries, were delivered in 1962 and 1966 respectively. However, the last of the very fast turbine steamers was the *Brighton*, which was built in 1950 and which was capable of making the 103 kilometre trip between Newhaven and Dieppe in just 210 minutes at a speed of 24 knots. Her turbines produced a total of 1,400 kilowatts.

The influence of Sir Charles Parsons on the short sea operations of Britain, and for that matter the rest of the world, could not have been foreseen when he negotiated his first contract with the military in the late-1890s. That contract was based on his earlier proven record to produce small amounts of power for use in remote lighting systems. The need for naval prowess, and for speed, provided the funds for the development of this innovative form of power, an early example of a military requirement supporting the development of a commercially important engineering concept.

There were a total of 131 coastal turbine steamers in the British registry. Figure 2 shows the uptake of the new engines in the Edwardian era, an uptake only inhibited by the war years with recovery nearly attained by the 1930s. No turbine steamers were actually completed during World War II although a number lay on the stocks. The arrival of the Pametrada design in the 1950s boosted numbers, but by then the internal combustion engine had become economically superior. Most of the steamers were passenger carriers: 14 were built for the excursion trade, 5 for overnight cattle and goods services, and the remainder for normal cross-channel duties.

All were purpose built save three which were converted from military origins, although one of these was originally built as a Canadian passenger steamer before adopting the title HMCS. All were built in the UK except the *Londres* (Chapter 12) which was built at Le Havre and was transferred from French registry late in her career. Without exception the ships served magnificently throughout much of the Twentieth Century and they made a major contribution to the national effort during two world wars. The vision of Mr Parsons must never be understated.

Sir Charles Algernon Parsons (1854-1931)

The youngest son of the third Earl of Rosse, Charles Parsons showed considerable talent for mathematics at Cambridge before going on to an engineering apprenticeship. In 1884 he became a junior partner in Clarke, Chapman & Company of Gateshead, where he invented the first steam turbine dynamo, capable of providing a ship's lighting system with up to 7.5 kilowatts. By 1889 he had set up his own company at Heaton where he produced the first turbo-dynamo for a land based power station, a principle still in use today. At the separate works of the Parsons Marine Steam Turbine Company at Wallsend he constructed the experimental steam torpedo boat *Turbinia*. Two years after the demonstration of the *Turbinia* to the Admiralty in 1897, the turbine destroyers HMS *Viper* and HMS *Cobra* were commissioned from Parsons. They attained record speeds of 36.6 knots using 8,500 kilowatts but, sadly, in 1901 the *Cobra* broke her back in heavy weather, due to her light construction.

Parsons went on to develop the geared turbine in 1909 at his Wallsend Turbinia Works and then developed the high pressure turbine used in the *King George V* in 1926. His other commercial interests included two optical glass companies. He was honoured as a Fellow of the Royal Society in 1898 and was awarded the Rumford and Copley Gold Medals. He was also a keen patron of the arts and was awarded the Albert Medal of the Royal Society of Arts.

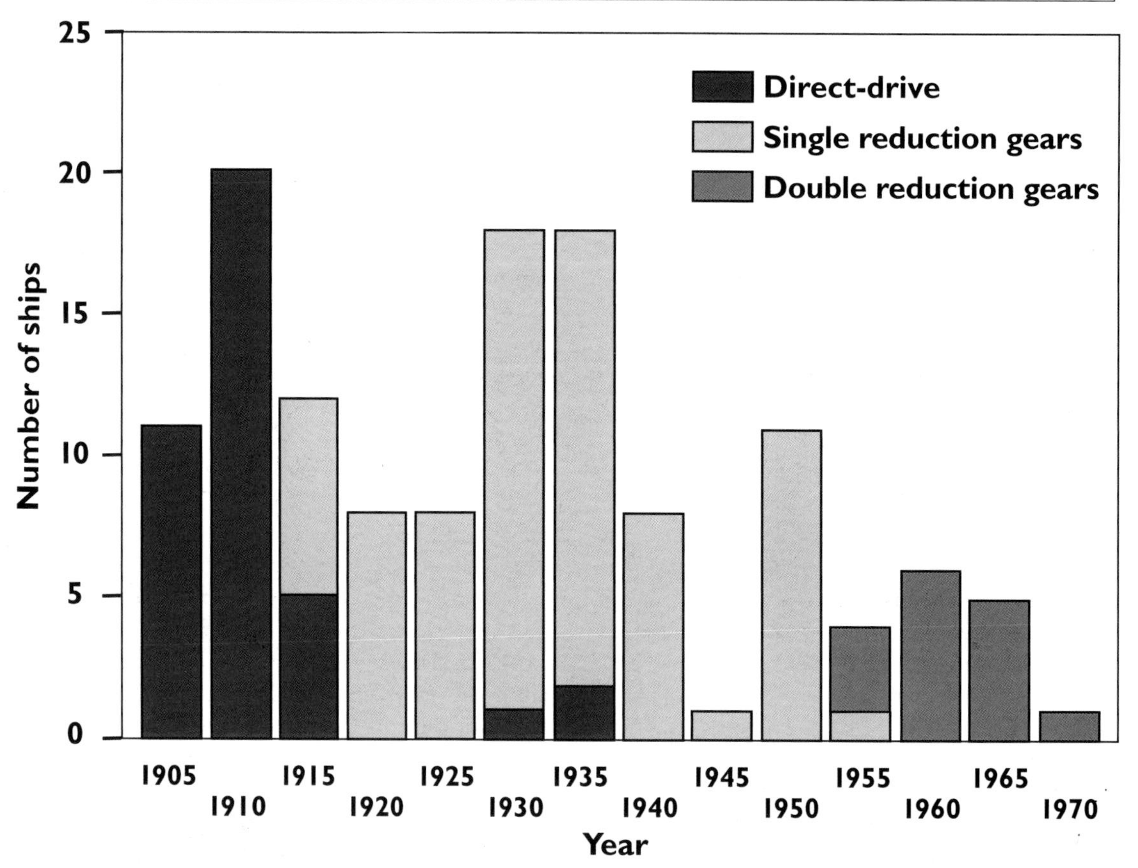

Figure 2.
Number of coastal turbine steamers built in the five year period prior to the year shown.

DIRECT-DRIVE TURBINE STEAMERS

The immediate success of *The Queen* on the Dover Strait lead to a succession of orders for direct-drive cross-channel turbine steamers. A total of 39 direct-drive turbine steamers were built for the British register (Table 1, page 25). With the exception of three excursion steamers, the last was built in 1912, as by 1911 the first of the single reduction geared turbine steamers had already been launched. Nearly half of the direct-drive steamers were built by William Denny at Dumbarton. All the ships had the same three shaft arrangement with the high pressure turbine coupled to the central shaft and the two low pressure turbines at the wings. Some of the later ships, such as the *Caesarea*, had the port propeller revolving in the opposite direction to the other two, in order to counter a tendency to yaw to starboard whilst travelling at speed.

The first two cross-channel turbine ships were *The Queen*, which was launched by Denny on 4th April 1903 and designed for the Dover and Folkestone stations, and the *Brighton* which followed from the same yard on 13th June for the Newhaven service. The order for *The Queen* was only placed on 29th November 1902, following the successful trials of the Clyde excursion steamer *Queen Alexandra* (see Chapter 1). *The Queen* ran her own trials in late May and undertook her maiden voyage to Calais on 29th June, just two days after being delivered. The *Brighton* was delivered seven weeks behind schedule in late August, and her builders were duly penalised £125 per week.

The Queen achieved nearly 22 knots on trials and was capable of 13 knots astern and could stop from 19 knots in 2½ ship lengths. Assistance in moving astern was provided by a bow rudder. She was 95 m long by 12 m broad. Her maiden commercial voyage from Dover to Calais was made outward in 53 minutes and back in 60. The ship was almost vibration free and quickly proved herself a good sea boat as in her first week of service it was reported that she was the only ship to arrive in Dover with dry decks during a day of 'sloppy' weather. Within two years of her delivery the South Eastern & Chatham Railway (the SE & C was affectionately known as the Slow Easy and Comfortless Railway!) had ordered two sisters. These were the *Onward* which was the motto of the South Eastern Railway, and the *Invicta* which was the motto of the other part of the Joint Committee, the London, Chatham & Dover Railway.

The *Victoria* and *Empress* followed in 1907 with more traditional 'royal' names. The *Victoria* arrived at Dover on 24th April, having travelled the 1,300 kilometres from the Clyde through rough conditions in 34 hours at a speed of 22.5 knots. She very quickly demonstrated her record breaking ability by crossing from Dover to Calais in just 46 minutes. The *Empress* was launched on 13th April and she took 33 hours to get down to Dover arriving on 9th June.

There were some slight outward differences between the five ships. For example, *The Queen* had her foremast clear of the deck saloon and the deck saloon had circular windows; the *Onward* had oblong windows to the deck saloon. These two ships were involved in an amazing incident on 30th May 1908. Under the command of Captain P Walker, the *Onward* left Folkestone 15 minutes behind schedule at 13.10 hours and 25 minutes later Captain C King took *The Queen* out of Boulogne. In a thick patch of fog in mid-channel the two collided head on; one man was killed when he fell and struck his head during the impact. Both ships were back in service within a month, when the

Dieppe (1905), leaving Newhaven Harbour on passage to Dieppe. (National Maritime Museum)

Onward had the privilege of carrying the first motor car across the Channel. The car was owned by a Mr Charles Jarrott and was carried under the auspices of the Automobile Association.

A delightful story tells how Captain George Blaxland, pre-World War I commodore of the fleet, was frustrated at damaging the rudder of the *Empress* against a concrete apron at Boulogne. He telephoned Dover for permission to return, albeit in flat calm conditions, stern first using his bow rudder to steer. Permission was granted and the voyage was made with an arrival time only 45 minutes behind schedule - curiously not one passenger remarked on this unusual procedure!

At Newhaven, the *Brighton* also created a stir on entry into service. The ship had cost £65,000 to build. She was followed in 1905 by an almost identical sister, the *Dieppe*, but which was built by Fairfields at Govan rather than by Denny.

It was the *Brighton* which, on the night of 6th November 1910, ran down the mighty six masted German sailing ship *Preussen* which was on passage from the Elbe to Valparaiso. A 5 m gash in the bow of the sailing ship cost the foremast and forward funnel of the steamer which had been cut away by the bowsprit of the sailing ship; the *Preussen* foundered in tow near Dover, whereas the *Brighton* safely put back to Newhaven.

In 1904 the next railway company to go turbine was the Midland Railway with the *Manxman* for the Isle of Man service and the *Londonderry* for the brand-new Belfast service using their newly completed port facilities at Heysham. The pair were designed by Sir John Biles and were slightly different in dimensions and had different boiler pressures, 10 bar for the *Manxman* and 14 bar for the *Londonderry*, although the former was nearly always a knot faster. Two further sisters, the *Antrim* and the *Donegal*, were equipped with conventional four cylinder triple expansion engines; it was found that the turbine ships had a slightly greater speed for slightly less fuel consumption, although actual figures are unclear. The four ships could each carry over 2,000 passengers. The *Manxman*, acclaimed as the fastest commercial ship afloat, lost this title after only one year to the Isle of Man Company's *Viking*

Manxman (1904), as built for the Midland Railway Heysham to Douglas service. (Malcolm McRonald collection)

and the Belgian *Princesse Elisabeth.*

At Stranraer, a new mail contract coupled with increased traffic led to the building of the *Princess Maud.* Another typical Denny product, she was launched on 20 February 1904 and delivered at the end of May to the Portpatrick and Wigtownshire Joint Railways Committee at a cost of £66,100. The mail service comprised a leisurely 06.00 hours departure from Stranraer, returning from Larne at 19.00 hours. Additional summer services were operated, plus Saturday and Sunday afternoon cruises from Larne to Rathlin Island and Bangor in County Down. It was even the custom in those days for the steamers to pass close by in mid-channel and greet each other with an exchange of two long blasts on their sirens, an event which many passengers came out on deck to witness.

Next came the first non-railway owned cross-channel turbine steamer, the Isle of Man Steam Packet Company's *Viking.* This magnificent ship was built at a cost of £83,900 with accommodation for 1,600 passengers against a crew complement of 80. She was designed in response to the new Midland Railway steamer *Manxman* and was guaranteed by her builders to be capable of one knot more than her competitor. Her registered speed was only 22 knots but she made 24 knots on a number of occasions and quickly established the record for the Fleetwood to Douglas crossing of 2 hours and 22 minutes with an average speed of over 23 knots. The ship was so successful that her owners received the new *Ben-my-Chree* in 1908 from the same builders. Launched on 23rd March, this new ship took her name from the Gaelic 'Bean mo Cridhe', meaning 'Wife of my Heart'. She could carry 2,550 passengers and had a crew complement of 119. Her cost was £112,000. Advertised at the time as "the fastest and most luxuriously appointed channel steamer afloat", her normal service speed on the main line Liverpool to Douglas service was 24 knots and she is said to have once attained nearly 27 knots. She did, however, consume up to 95 tons of coal in a day. Sadly a war loss, this record breaker was bombed and sunk in 1917.

In August 1905 the Caledonian Steam Packet Company placed an order with William Denny for

Ben-my-Chree on acceptance trials in 1908. (John Shepherd collection)

a turbine steamer which was to be 76 m long by 9 m broad, almost identical in size to the original turbine steamer, the *King Edward*. This was the *Duchess of Argyll*, designed for the fast commuter runs on the lower Clyde. The response from the Glasgow & South Western Railway was to invite tenders for the construction of either a duplicate of their paddle steamer *Mars* of 1902, or, radically, a turbine steamer. In the end, an offer from John Brown to build a turbine steamer for £21,000 was accepted. The new ship, the *Atalanta*, had the same dimensions as the *Mars* and was 64 m long with a beam of 9 m; her length to breadth ratio was a stubby 7.0, whereas that of the *King Edward* was 8.4 (*The Queen* and her sisters on the Dover Strait had a ratio of 7.7).

The *Atalanta* was never an entirely successful ship, but managed her design speed of 18 knots with ease although she was reboilered at the end of her first season. Widespread belief at the time was that John Brown had already constructed the engines before the tender was issued. The engines could have been scaled down versions of those installed later in the Cunard Liners *Carmania* and *Lusitania*, and built to provide the Clydeside engineers with experience of the new technology. If true, this could account for why the little ship was so beamy; she was in any case never a good sea boat.

The *Duchess of Argyll* was intended to be named 'Marchioness of Graham', but Denny had her ready before the Marquis had married his intended, the Lady Mary Hamilton. The ship cost £30,000 to build and was the sixteenth turbine ship to come from Denny's yard. Her length to breadth ratio was a more conventional 8.3 and she managed over 21 knots on trials before taking up station between Ardrossan and Brodick the next day, on 9th May 1906.

During 1905, the South Eastern & Chatham Railway placed the *Invicta* along with the paddle steamer *Empress* on day excursions from Margate to Boulogne. This was a serious challenge to the General Steam Navigation Company who then monopolised these routes, and that company responded by ordering a turbine steamer of their own from Dennys. This was the *Kingfisher*, some 8 m longer than the *King Edward*, but capable of over 21 knots. Her Promenade Deck extended all the way to the bows and was plated up beneath. The new ship was put into service with Tilbury as her base, picking up passengers from the lower Thames ports for Boulogne or non-landing Channel cruises. Sadly, she was not a success; she was a very expensive unit to employ on seasonal work, perhaps too big for the excursion trade but too small for cross-channel work, and she was sold to Italian owners in 1911.

The Great Central Railway brought out a pair of modestly powered ships in 1906, the *Immingham* and the *Marylebone,* for the nightly Grimsby to Rotterdam service. Their design speed was 18 knots, and they were found to be expensive units to run in opposition to the nightly service out of Harwich, operated by the Great Eastern Railway. Although they reduced the voyage by 7 hours to just over 10 hours, both ships were re-engined in 1911 with triple expansion engines and given single screws (and single funnels), so reducing their speed to an even more modest 13 knots. The service was not resumed after the Great War, the *Immingham* having been lost at the Dardanelles, and the *Marylebone* transferred to the Tilbury to Antwerp service of the Great Eastern Railway.

An important quartet came next for the Fishguard & Rosslare Railways and Harbour Company and represented a total investment of £440,000. In 1898 the Great Western Railway and the Great Southern and Western Railway, which operated out of Dublin, agreed to prepare for a new service to operate between Fishguard and Rosslare as direct competition to the Holyhead to Kingstown mail route. The engineering work for the two new harbours was colossal, and three fast steamers were commissioned from John Brown, each carrying the name of the patron saint of one of the participating countries: *St David, St George* and *St Patrick.* Used on both day and night services, the ships could accommodate 562 first and 438 second class passengers, with sleeping berths for over 400 first class passengers. The ships had two full length decks, apart from the boiler rooms on the Lower Deck, a 15 m forecastle and a long Boat Deck. They had three cargo holds, one of which was insulated for the carriage of refrigerated goods. They were constructed with a cellular double bottom and there was a deep tank which could take up to 160 tons of

Immingham (1906) as built, before her turbine engines were replaced by conventional steam reciprocating engines. (National Maritime Museum)

St George (1906), as she appeared when first built for service at Fishguard. (Glasgow University)

water. All the winches were electric.

The new route opened on 30th August 1906 but it was soon realised that a fourth ship would help maintain the service so the *St Andrew*, an almost identical sister, joined the trio in 1908. The service required departures from Fishguard at 02.15 and 14.15 hours, and from Rosslare at 11.30 and 23.45 hours. The four ships had a length to breadth ratio of 8.6 to 8.9. They had eight single-ended three-furnace boilers which provided steam at 13 bar. The bunkers held about 170 tons of coal.

The *St George* was sold for service in Canada in May 1913, as traffic had fallen off considerably by then. However, she returned to Britain during the war and was then bought by the Great Eastern Railway to supplement the overnight Harwich to Hook of Holland service. For this she was altered to carry only 498 passengers. Displaced by new tonnage in 1929 she was then sold for demolition. However, the *St David* and *St Patrick* were re-engined in 1925 and 1926 respectively, by John Brown & Company, with single reduction geared turbines. The *St Patrick* only lasted until 1929 when she was declared a constructive total loss after a fire at Fishguard. Her engines were salvaged and passed on to the *St Andrew*. The two surviving saints were themselves displaced in 1933, and sold for scrap. These were the only attempts to re-engine direct-drive cross-channel ships with single reduction geared equipment.

The only turbine steamer ever to be built for any of the companies later to be amalgamated into the Coast Lines Seaway, and their express passenger services between mainland Britain and Ireland, was the *Viper*. She was designed for G & J Burns' daylight service between Ardrossan and Belfast, and her maiden voyage on the route took place on 1st June 1906. The new ship had a service speed of 22 knots; she was 3 knots faster than her predecessor on the route. She was a very impressive vessel, with two well-raked black funnels which gave her an appearance of power; able to carry 1,700 passengers she required a crew of 60. On her bow was a golden viper coiling on the bulwarks.

The *Viper* had an exceptionally powerful astern turbine and was capable of 18 knots in reverse. This, coupled with a bow rudder, enabled her to swing inbound off Carrickfergus and travel stern first up the channel to Belfast.

Thus, at the end of 1906 and in the space of

only three years, the turbine had colonised the prestigious services out of Dover and Folkestone, as well as the rival service at Newhaven. Turbine steamers had inaugurated two main line Irish services from the brand new railway ports at Heysham and Fishguard (and Rosslare), and had introduced radically reduced crossing times on a number of daylight sailings elsewhere. The Edwardian ships had already acquired a reputation for speed, reliability and comfort that was previously unknown. With the possible exception of the *Atalanta*, and also the *Immingham* and *Marylebone* which were not ideally economically suited to their design service out of Grimsby, all the direct-drive steamers were a great success.

It was concluded at that time that the turbine was a vastly superior engine to the reciprocating engine. A contemporary review by Sir Alexander Richardson, states that ships such as *The Queen*, the *Onward* and the *Invicta* could carry a greater payload at higher speed, with considerable reduction in maintenance cost and with about one quarter less consumption of coal than conventional reciprocating engined ships.

Aware of the obvious merits of the turbine steamer, the Great Eastern Railway placed orders with John Brown for two ships for delivery in 1907 for the Harwich to Hook of Holland service. These were the *Copenhagen*, which undertook her maiden voyage on 22nd October 1907, and the *Munich*, which followed down the slipway on 26th August 1908. They were big ships, 105 m long with a beam of 13 m; their service speed was 20 knots.

The new Harwich-Hook ships were luxurious units with accommodation for 450 passengers in two classes; there was widespread use of mahogany and maplewood with blood-red drapes in the public areas. All cabins, both for passengers and crew, had telephones, and the ships had wireless communication systems. The success of these ships led to a third, the *St Petersburg*, being delivered also from John Brown with maiden voyage on 7th July 1910. The new ships displaced two older vessels and replaced the *Berlin* which was tragically lost in a storm on 21st February 1907, when she struck the West Pier at the entrance to the New Waterway with the loss of 128 lives. The two surviving sisters of the *Berlin* were transferred to the Belgian service on the arrival of the turbine ships.

Another company aware of the tremendous benefits of the turbine engine was the Joint Committee of the Lancashire and Yorkshire and the London & North Western Railways who operated the Fleetwood to Belfast night service. At a cost of £85,000 each, William Denny built the *Duke of Cumberland* and the *Duke of Argyll*. They were launched on 14th May and 25th June 1909 respectively, the former managing 22 knots on trials, the latter slightly less. Their increased speed on service reduced the crossing time by half an hour.

The accommodation of the two new 'Dukes' was said to be second to none, with first class (saloon accommodation) of two- and four-berth cabins amidships and second class (steerage) aft, although sleeping berths in steerage were only available to the drovers accompanying cattle shipments. There was special four-berth accommodation for unaccompanied lady travellers, but men had the preserve of their own smoking room. Overflow accommodation was curtained off in the dining saloon where temporary bunks allowed their inmates the pleasure of listening to the stewards preparing the dining room for breakfast! However, immediately after the war in 1919 the Fleetwood service was wound up due to falling passenger numbers in the years leading up to the partitioning of Ireland.

The Channel Island service of the London & South Western Railway was next to receive turbine steamers. These were the *Caesarea* and the *Sarnia* (respectively the Roman names for Jersey and Guernsey). These ships had a service speed of over 20 knots, they were 87 m long by 12 m broad and could carry 980 passengers. They were found to be expensive units to maintain on the service and were used as summer only ships, being laid up alongside each other in Southampton Water for much of the year.

A number of the early turbine steamers, including the *Caesarea*, were to find their way into the service of the Isle of Man Steam Packet

Company which adopted a policy after the First World War of buying second-hand railway tonnage. These were the *Manxman*, formerly of the Midland Railway and bought from the Admiralty at the end of World War I and which came into the Manx fleet without change of name, the *Onward*, which despite being scuttled after being set on fire by an incendiary device at Folkestone in April 1918, became the *Mona's Isle*, and the *Viper* which was bought for £60,000 and renamed *Snaefell*, all in 1920. The *Caesarea* was purchased for only £9,000 in November 1923 and given the name *Manx Maid*; she had previously hit the rocks and partially sank off the south coast of Jersey that year, was salvaged and towed to Southampton to await sale. The old *Victoria* was also acquired without change of name in 1928 for £28,000. The latter vessel survived being mined during World War Two and supported the company until the 1956 season after which, at the grand age of 50, she was sold for demolition at Barrow. The *Manxman*, the *Mona's Isle* and the *Snaefell* all survived the two world wars and were sold for breaking up between 1948 and 1950, a tribute to their builders and their engines.

The South Eastern & Chatham Railway took delivery of two further ships of *The Queen* class: the *Riviera*, launched from Denny on 1st April 1911, and the *Engadine*, which followed on 23 September at a combined cost of £167,600. Both ships had slightly greater power than the original quintet and this enabled them to maintain the Dover to Calais service with a crossing time of 60 minutes. They also had deck space specially set aside for the carriage of motor cars.

The last of the direct-drive cross-Channel steamers were the *Greenore*, built for the Holyhead to Greenore service of the London & North Western Railway, and the *Princess Victoria*, for the Portpatrick & Wigtownshire Joint Railway Committee. Both ships were delivered in 1912. The *Greenore* could carry 950 passengers on her secondary route, but as the service was closed in 1926, the ship was then sold for demolition. She could maintain a speed of over 20 knots and her powerful astern turbine could stop the vessel from full speed in just 280 m. The highlight of her career was maintaining the prestigious Holyhead to Dublin route during the war years when her big sisters were away on Admiralty service.

The *Princess Victoria* was essentially a sister of the old *Princess Maud*, one of the very first batch of Denny-built turbine steamers. She had the traditional arrangement of saloon accommodation amidships, and steerage aft, with movable stalls for livestock on the Lower Deck. The saloon accommodation included a dining saloon on the Main Deck and a smoke room and ladies room on the Promenade Deck. The older ship maintained the Stranraer-Larne service during the war, usually with two crossings per day, whereas the *Princess Victoria* moved south to act as a cross-channel troopship out of Southampton and only returned to her commercial service in 1920. The *Princess Maud* ended her days after striking Barr's Point near Larne on 9th June 1931 in dense fog; the 300 passengers were safely landed in the ship's boats, but the ship herself was deemed unworthy of repair and was sold for demolition. Her sister followed her to the breakers' yard three years later on the arrival of new tonnage.

There remained three further direct-drive turbine steamers yet to be built and destined for excursion use (See Chapter 5).

The war service of many of these early ships was exemplary. Seven of the ships were actually lost to enemy action, three in World War I, the remainder in World War II. There are many stories that can be recounted and these are best summarised by that of *The Queen* on 26th October 1914. Having delivered a full load of troops at Boulogne, this marvellous ship was returning home under the command of Captain R E Carey with a King's Messenger, some British officers, American Red Cross Officials, a member of the Press and a handful of nurses aboard. They soon came across the steamer *Amiral Ganteaume* carrying some 2,500 French and Belgian refugees to Le Havre, but she was lying low in the water and flying the distress signal. It was clearly too rough to launch the ship's boats and Captain Carey decided that his only course of action was to come alongside. He managed to bring *The Queen* up astern of the other

Princess Maud (1904) was the first turbine steamer to operate on the Irish services. (Glasgow University)

ship so that many of the refugees could scramble across the heaving gap to safety. Although some perished between the ships, and desperate parents threw their young across the gap to willing hands, a second circuit along the lee side enabled *The Queen* to take 2,200 people off the stricken ship.

Returning to Folkestone in squally weather, one desperate girl had to have both legs amputated on deck and she then gave birth to a baby girl - both survived. There were 87 amputations that night, 11 births, and one further death. Captain and crew were thanked by the King when he visited the ship a few weeks later, and messages were also received from the French and Belgian Governments. The seamanship displayed that day undoubtedly reflected the qualities of the ship.

In post war years, the direct-drive turbine ships continued to serve throughout the 1920s, many into the 1930s and a few beyond. Several of the ships were converted from coal to oil burners in the 1920s and 1930s. Others changed hands: the *Engadine* became a Thames pleasure cruiser for the 1932 season before taking up service in the Philippines. The *Riviera* was sold to Burns & Laird in 1932 as the *Lairds Isle* for the Ardrossan to Belfast daylight service. After conversion to oil burning she survived yet another war, this time on the Dover Patrol and was finally retired from the Belfast service in 1957 at the age of 46.

The Fleetwood to Belfast service, later owned by the London, Midland & Scottish Railway, transferred the *Duke of Argyll* under the French flag to the newly formed Angleterre-Lorraine-Alsace Steamship Company in conjunction with the Chemin de Fer du Nord. Renamed *Alsacien* she inaugurated a new service between Tilbury and Dunkirk on 14th May 1927 along with the Heysham steamer *Londonderry* which was renamed *Flamand*. Shortly afterwards, they were joined by the *Picard*, formerly the *Duke of Cumberland*. The new service moved to Folkestone in 1932, and the older ships were successively withdrawn: the *Picard* to the Greek registry, but surviving in service at least until 1940, whilst the *Alsacien* and the *Flamand* were broken up in 1936.

The longest surviving ship was the *Duchess of Argyll*. She was employed as a cross-Channel troop carrier in World War I, and as a troopship tender in between her normal ferry duties on the Clyde in World War II. Her commercial role at an end, she was then used at Portland as a floating laboratory until she was eventually sold by the Admiralty for demolition in 1970. There were seven other direct-drive steamers which actually remained in commercial service into the 1950s, and the most remarkable career of all must be that of the Isle of Man Steam Packet Company's *Viking*, which must have payed for herself many times over, along with the *Victoria* and her half sister the *Riviera*, later the *Lairds Isle*.

The first aircraft carriers

The success of the Great Eastern Railway's three steamers, the *Copenhagen, Munich* and *St Petersburg*, led to the order of a fourth sister, but this time equipped with twin screws and single reduction gears. This was the *Stockholm* which was launched from the yard of John Brown on 9th June 1917; having been taken over by the Admiralty in February 1917, she was completed as an aircraft carrier and given the classical name HMS *Pegasus*. Conversion of a number of direct-drive turbine steamers had taken place earlier on in the war: the *Manxman* from the Midland Railway and the *Ben-my-Chree* and *Viking* (renamed HMS *Vindex* for the duration of the war) from the Isle of Man Steam Packet Company, plus the South Eastern & Chatham Railway's *Engadine, Riviera, Empress* and a Tasmanian ferry the *Nairana*. The *Engadine, Riviera* and *Nairana* were not fully converted and did not have a forward hangar and runway; they carried nine seaplanes between them: five Type 74s, two 'Folders' and two Type 135s, all Short aircraft which were lowered to the sea for take-off. These three ships set sail on 21st December 1914 to attack the Zeppelin sheds at Cuxhaven. The subsequent Christmas Day raid was not a success and was foiled by fog and the failure of two of the planes to get off the water.

Hangars were constructed forward and aft of the funnels on the other ships, and the masts were paired, one on either side of the ship. Three planes were housed in the forward hangar which led to a sloping 'runway' over the bow. A large gantry was built over the stern with a crane on either side. A section of the aft runway could slide away to allow planes to be lifted from the sea onto the runway. HMS *Pegasus* and HMS *Vindex* could carry Bristol Scout fighter planes which were powered by 60 kilowatt Gnome engines, the others mainly carried seaplanes which had wheeled trolleys, jettisoned after take off. The vessels required a crew of some 250, including flying crews and mechanics. The fighter planes were equipped with flotation bags which enabled them to land on the sea; the first ever take off from a ship took place on 5th November 1915 from the forward flight deck of HMS *Vindex*.

The ship would head into the wind for take off, using speed as necessary. A plane would rev up whilst a hook held it steady until it was released down the sloping 30 m long runway over the bows. If the pilot could not gain sufficient lift his plane would fall into the sea and was likely to be rammed by the ship seconds later. This was a precarious business as the converted steamers had considerably greater top hamper than their original design specification, and this vast windage, coupled with their shallow draft, made them difficult to handle in variable winds. The runway on the *Ben-my-Chree* was only 20 m long but this proved inadequate for the planes, so in practice, the ship had to stop and lower the seaplanes to the water for take off. The three partially converted carriers also had to adopt this same procedure, and this process made them all very vulnerable. The *Ben-my-Chree* carried four Short 184 seaplanes which were powered with a 170 kilowatt Sunbeam engine. The crew of two had a radio, a Lewis gun and one 355 mm torpedo. It was one of these planes, piloted by Flight Commander C H Edmonds, which sunk a Turkish supply ship on 12th August 1915, the first successful airborne torpedo attack on record.

Table 1 : Direct-drive turbine steamers built between 1901 and 1912

	Owner	year built	scrapped /lost	tons gross	power+ (kilowatts)	speed (knots)	builder
King Edward*	Turbine Steamers Limited	1901	1952	562		20	William Denny
Queen Alexandra*	Turbine Steamers Limited	1902				21	William Denny
Brighton	London, Brighton & South Coast Railway	1903	1933	1,129	4,400	21	William Denny
The Queen	South Eastern & Chatham Railway	1903	1916	1,676	5,600	21	William Denny
Londonderry	Midland Railway	1904	1936	2,086	4,700	22	William Denny
Manxman	Midland Railway	1904	1949	2,086	4,700	22	Vickers Sons & Maxim
Princess Maud	Portpatrick & Wigtownshire Joint Railway	1904	1932	1,746		20	William Denny
Dieppe	London, Brighton & South Coast Railway	1905	1941	1,210	4,400	21	Fairfield S & E
Invicta	South Eastern & Chatham Railway	1905	1933	1,680	5,600	21	William Denny
Onward	South Eastern & Chatham Railway	1905	1948	1,671	5,600	21	William Denny
Viking	Isle of Man Steam Packet Company	1905	1954	1,957	8,200	22	Armstrong Whitworth
Atalanta	Glasgow & South Western Railway	1906	1945	486		17	John Brown
Duchess of Argyll	Caledonian Steam Packet Company	1906	1970	594		20	William Denny
Immingham	Great Central Railway	1906	1915	2,009		18	Swan Hunter
Kingfisher*	General Steam Navigation Company	1906	1938	982		20	William Denny
Marylebone	Great Central Railway	1906	1938	1,972		18	Cammell Laird
St David•	Fishguard & Rosslare Railways and Harbour Co	1906	1933	2,529	7,500	20	John Brown
St George	Fishguard & Rosslare Railways and Harbour Co	1906	1929	2,456	7,500	20	Cammell Laird
St Patrick•	Fishguard & Rosslare Railways and Harbour Co	1906	1929	2,531	7,500	20	John Brown
Victoria	South Eastern & Chatham Railway	1906	1957	1,689	5,600	21	William Denny
Viper	G & J Burns	1906	1948	1,713	5,200	21	Fairfield S & E
Empress	South Eastern & Chatham Railway	1907	1933	1,690	5,200	22	William Denny
Copenhagen	Great Eastern Railway	1907	1917	2,570	7,500	20	John Brown
Munich	Great Eastern Railway	1907	1950	2,570	7,500	20	John Brown
Ben-my-Chree	Isle of Man Steam Packet Company	1908	1917	2,250	10,400	24	Vickers Sons & Maxim
St Andrew•	Fishguard & Rosslare Railways and Harbour Co	1908	1933	2,528	7,500	20	John Brown
Duke of Argyll	Lancashire & Yorkshire/London & North Western Railway	1909	1936	2,052	6,300	22	William Denny
Duke of Cumberland	Lancashire & Yorkshire/London & North Western Railway	1909	1939	2,052	6,300	19	William Denny
Caesarea	London & South Western Railway	1910	1950	1,505	4,500	20	Cammell Laird
Sarnia	London & South Western Railway	1910	1918	1,498	4,500	20	Cammell Laird
St Petersburg	Great Eastern Railway	1910	1941	2,570		20	John Brown
Engadine	South Eastern & Chatham Railway	1911	1941	1,676	6,000	22	William Denny
Riviera	South Eastern & Chatham Railway	1911	1957	1,674	6,000	20	William Denny
Greenore	London & North Western Railway	1912	1926	1,488		20	Cammell Laird
Princess Victoria	Portpatrick & Wigtownshire Joint Railway	1912	1934	1,678		19	William Denny
Queen Alexandra*	Turbine Steamers Limited	1912	1958	785		20	William Denny

* excursion steamer +shaft or indicated power •later re-engined and converted to single reduction gears

EARLY GEARED TURBINE STEAMERS

The economic problem of running a high speed direct-drive turbine engine on services such as Grimsby to Rotterdam or the Channel Islands, on which speed was not essential, was resolved with the introduction of the single reduction geared turbine. Although Parsons had proved the viability of the geared turbine with his experiments at Wallsend in 1909, the engineering difficulties of excessive wear on the gears and chaffing of the turbine blades took some time to overcome. The single reduction geared turbine comprised a pair of expansion turbines, commonly a high and low pressure plus a reversing turbine, which were coupled to two independent shafts via single reduction gearing.

The first cross-channel steamer to be equipped with the higher speed turbines and twin screws coupled by single reduction gears was the *Normannia*. She was built for the London & South Western Railway by Fairfield Shipbuilding & Engineering at Govan, and was designed for the long run between Southampton and Le Havre. The ship was launched on 9th November 1911 and cost £71,500 to build. Not only was her machinery unique but her external appearance was also original. Her superstructure was fully enclosed allowing full use to be made of deck space for the public rooms, but most distinctive of all was her cruiser stern. A sister ship, the *Hantonia* was launched on 23rd December originally with the name *Louvima*. The after part of the Main Deck was enclosed in both ships during the 1930s.

Normannia (1911) at Le Havre. She was the first steamer to be equipped with single reduction gears.

(Kevin Le Scelleur collection)

Hantonia (1911), approaching St Helier in the summer of 1923. (Kevin Le Scelleur collection)

The sisters had a gross tonnage of 1,567. Their service speed was just over 19 knots and they required a crew of 50. Both ships were highly successful, maintaining the service they were designed for, with occasional duties on the Channel Islands routes. During the two wars they were extensively used for trooping; the *Normannia* was lost off Dunkerque in 1940. Her sister survived and was finally withdrawn from the Le Havre route in 1952, after 41 years service. She remained a coal burner to the end.

A third ship was ordered in 1914, this time from William Denny. Although intended as one of a pair, the war prevented work ever starting on the second ship and halted work on the first. She was eventually launched in December 1918 as the *Lorina*, and she entered service as a cross-Channel troopship. Released by the Admiralty only four months later, the *Lorina* was able to take up duty on the Southampton to St Malo and Channel Islands services in March 1920. Alas, she too was lost at Dunkerque.

The third twin screw cross-Channel turbine steamer to enter service was the *Paris*, built for the Newhaven to Dieppe service of the London, Brighton & South Coast Railway by William Denny. This was a magnificent vessel capable of nearly 25 knots and equipped with one of the most powerful sets of turbines ever to be installed in a cross-Channel ship. Eight Yarrow boilers produced steam at 66 bar, and the twin turbine units generated 10,400 shaft kilowatts. She could accommodate 960 passengers and required a crew of 42. A near sister, the *Versailles*, was built in France and completed in 1919 to the order of the Chemin de Fer de l'Ouest. The *Paris* was reboilered in 1931 and converted to oil burning; this cost over £33,000, in a ship which had been built originally for only £81,300. She was also lost at Dunkerque, whilst the *Versailles* survived, only to be scrapped in 1946.

The Isle of Man Steam Packet Company was also keen to take up the new technology. Their first single reduction geared turbine ship was the *King Orry*. The ship and the engines were built by Cammell Laird at Birkenhead at a cost of £96,000. She had a gross tonnage of 1,877 and could accommodate 1,600 passengers with a crew of 60.

Lorina (1918), as built. She served the Southampton to St Malo and Channel Islands routes between the wars.
(Kevin Le Scelleur collection)

King Orry (1913) was a product of Cammell Laird at Birkenhead. It is seen here with a full load of holiday makers.
(Malcolm McRonald collection)

She was found to be a most economical ship, with a service speed of 20 knots, and could easily make 21 knots if necessary. She suffered the ignominy of a stranding at New Brighton in 1921, amazingly without any structural damage. She was extensively overhauled in 1934 and converted to oil burning in 1939. Present at the surrender of the German Fleet in the Firth of Forth in November 1918, she too was another casualty of the Dunkerque evacuation in May 1940.

Three more turbine steamers were to be completed before the outbreak of war. The first was the pleasure steamer *St Seiriol*. Built in 1914, to the order of the Liverpool & North Wales Steamship Company by A & J Inglis, she was immediately taken over by the Admiralty and used as a troopship out of Southampton, before conversion to minesweeping duties. In this capacity she was lost off Harwich in April 1918. She was small relative to the cross-channel ships of the day being 73 m long with a beam of 9 m, and her gross tonnage was only 927.

Two more ships to be ordered before the onset of hostilities were the *Biarritz* and *Maid of Orleans*. They were designed to partner the first cross-Channel turbine steamers, *The Queen*, and her seven consorts. As it happened, only the *Biarritz* was delivered before the war; the *Maid of Orleans* was not launched until March 1918 as her turbines had been commandeered by the Navy. These ships were larger than their predecessors, with a gross tonnage of 2,495 and 2,384 respectively. Although they were born at troubled times, they were successful ships which served their owners well. They could carry 1,330 passengers and could maintain the Dover Strait crossing with a service speed of 23 knots. A highlight occurred on New Year's Day in 1923 when the *Biarritz* carried King George V and his Queen to Boulogne on a state visit. The ship had an escort of nine destroyers, and she flew the White Ensign and the Admiralty Flag at the fore and the Royal Standard at the main. In May 1924 the *Maid of Orleans* was host to the King and Queen of Rumania and the Italian Royal family.

In 1925 both ships were extensively upgraded and converted to burn oil fuel. In keeping with many other short sea vessels their Lower Deck was plated-in, considerably altering their appearance. Happily, both ships were to survive Dunkerque, although the *Biarritz* was hit by shell fire, and the *Maid of Orleans* was involved in collision with HMS *Worcester* after rescuing over 5,000 men in six trips. The captain of the *Maid of Orleans*, Captain G D Walker, was subsequently awarded the DSC. The *Maid of Orleans* was later torpedoed with the loss of five men, after leaving the Normandy beaches as part of Group J4 on 28th June 1944. The explosion totally disintegrated one of the landing craft suspended from her davits, and a plume of spray shot to twice the height of the bridge.

The *Biarritz* later retired from the Harwich to Hook troop run in 1949 to be broken up on the beach at Dover. Throughout the commercial career of the *Biarritz*, she sported a plaque which read "*Breslau*, January 20, 1918" and which contained drawings by her former mining officer Lieutenant St John Cracroft-Encotts. This commemorated her part in the mining of the *Breslau* and damage caused to the German battle cruiser *Goeben* in the Aegean Sea.

The last pre-war order for a turbine driven cross-channel steamer was placed in 1914 with William Denny by the London & North Western Railway. Intended for the Holyhead - North of Ireland service to Greenore, the ship was to be a quasi-sister of the direct-drive turbine steamer *Greenore* (Chapter 2) and the triple expansion piston-engined steamer *Rathmore*, dating from 1908. The new ship was eventually launched on 30th April 1919, completed at a cost of £98,500, and was given the name *Curraghmore*. She had an attractive profile, with two evenly spaced masts and two funnels, and she was the only ship ever built for the company with a cruiser stern. She had accommodation for 495 first class passengers amidships and 580 steerage passengers aft. Berths were available for 172 passengers, of which 14 were for the exclusive use of cattle drovers.

When she finally took up station at Holyhead, she was loaned to the City of Dublin Company who then held the mail contract but had lost two of its ships in the war. When the mail contract was won by her owners in 1920, she was transferred to this service before new tonnage (the *Anglia* and *Hibernia*, see below) displaced her onto the route for which she was designed. At last, the Greenore service sported its three new purpose-built ships, the *Curraghmore, Greenore* and the *Rathmore* and there were great expectations of the southern rail and sea route from London through to Belfast.

Trouble was brewing in Ireland at that time, and the Greenore service was particularly vulnerable because of the geographical location of the Irish terminal. With the confirmation of the Irish Treaty by the Dail in 1922, the partitioning of Ireland meant that the service had to cross a customs barrier between Holyhead and Greenore, and this made it immediately subordinate to the alternative route between Heysham and Belfast. Of course, in 1923, the grouping of the railways put both the Holyhead and Heysham services under the same banner, so that the competing Midland Railway was now also a part of the newly formed London, Midland and Scottish Railway. Inevitably, the Greenore service was to close, and in 1926 the entire passenger fleet was withdrawn leaving only a weekly cargo service.

The *Curraghmore*, now only seven years old, was retained as spare ship at Holyhead. It was not uncommon for the Welsh voices of the ship's talented choir to serenade the arriving passengers as they assembled on the quayside. Sadly, it was not long before the ship was transferred to Heysham under the name *Duke of Abercorn*. Here, she supported the new Dukes then being introduced on this service and which were immediately very popular (See Chapter 4). The *Duke of Abercorn* was considered, by the travelling public, to be a poor relative of the new ships and, at the tender age of 16, she was herself displaced by new tonnage, withdrawn and sold for a mere £5,000 for demolition.

The coveted Holyhead to Kingstown mail contract which was awarded to the London & North Western Railway in 1920 was valued at £100,000, a price that undercut the City of Dublin Company by 30%. The contract required two sailings per day, with a voyage time of 2 hours and 45 minutes from the Admiralty Pier at Holyhead, or 2 hours and 55 minutes from the Inner Harbour. It also stipulated transfer times of the mails between ship and train: 30 minutes at Holyhead, 15 minutes at Kingstown (five minutes less on the daytime sailing), and there was a penalty for each hour of delay.

Four ships had been ordered before the war, from William Denny, and these were redesigned for the mail service. The first two hulls had largely been completed and were being equipped as minelayers before the end of the war, but they were stripped out and completed for their original civilian purpose. The ships were given the traditional names of the four kingdoms: *Anglia, Hibernia, Cambria* and *Scotia*. They were nearly twice the size of their former namesakes, with a gross tonnage of 3,467, and they had a service speed of 25 knots derived from turbines with a total shaft power of 16,000 kilowatts, fed by a series of nine coal fired water-tube boilers. They could each maintain 23 knots on eight boilers. This allowed the ships considerable margin over the contract requirements should the boat trains be delayed or the weather be inclement. The cost of the ships was approximately £400,000 each. The quartet had an unusually high standard of accommodation: 936 first class passengers and 569 third class. They had a crew of 80, including 22 catering staff.

The ships were 116 m long and could not swing at Holyhead in the Inner Harbour. Consequently, they were equipped with a bow rudder, an after navigating bridge and navigating lights which enabled them to leave Holyhead stern first and turn in the Outer Harbour. They were imposing looking ships which had a slightly narrower forward funnel which gave them an appearance of power when viewed from ahead. On the afternoon of 27th November, the Irish steamer *Munster* carried the mails into Kingstown. Twelve hours later, in the early hours of 28th November, the *Anglia* sailed for Holyhead and for the first time the railway company was responsible for the delivery of the mail all the way from Ireland to London.

The transfer of the steamers to the London,

Cambria (1920), preparing for departure from the Inner Harbour at Holyhead. (Mike Walker collection)

Midland & Scottish Railway in 1923 led to a realisation that two steamers in service, one with banked fires ready to step in should there be a problem, and one off under maintenance, was indeed extravagant. As it happened, it was the turn of the *Anglia* for withdrawal for maintenance, so it was she that was laid-up at Holyhead and later moved to more permanent isolation at Barrow, ultimately to be broken up after ten years idleness - an ill fitting fate for such an advanced ship.

The other three ships were extensively reconditioned in 1932, when the forward 16 m of the Promenade Deck was plated in, and a new and spacious lounge provided below the bridge. Competition on the route eventually arrived in earnest during 1938 from the Liverpool - Dublin service which had then received the new motor ships *Leinster* and *Munster*. These ships quickly started to offer an attractive alternative to the now ageing steamships on the Holyhead route, and a contract was placed with Fairfield Shipbuilding & Engineering for two new 5,000 ton turbine steamers for the Holyhead route. The onset of World War II, however, led to the inevitable dissolution of this contract.

The *Scotia* was yet another casualty at Dunkerque. Under the command of Captain W Hughes, she had loaded 2,000 French troops when she received a bomb in the boiler room via the after funnel, from a dive bomber and a second bomb in the engine room via the casing. Some 300 men died including 32 crew members. Her two remaining sisters survived the war and were scrapped on the arrival of the new motor ships.

Planned before the Great War, but ordered at a later date, the trio *Bruges, Antwerp* and *Malines* were all built for the Great Eastern Railway service between Harwich and Antwerp. These were the last railway ships to be ordered before the grouping of the railway companies into the 'big four' (see Chapter 4). The new ships were 98 m long by 13 m broad and had a gross tonnage of just under 3,000. They each had four sets of turbines with steam generated by eight boilers which were oil fired. There were five conventional holds, and they were the first Harwich steamers to sport the fashionable cruiser stern. They could accommodate 1,250 passengers and had berths for 263 first and 100 second class passengers. The crew complement was 60.

The first two ships were products of John Brown, and they were delivered in March and July 1920. The *Malines* was launched on 6th January 1921 from the yard of Armstrong Whitworth on the Tyne and, following considerable delays over the installation of her machinery, she finally took up station at Harwich in late March 1922. The three ships maintained the Antwerp service and regularly stood in as reliefs on the Hook of Holland service. At the beginning of World War II, the *Malines* was sent to Rotterdam along with the *Munich*, now named *St Denis* (Chapter 2), to evacuate British citizens following the German invasion of Holland. Both were still in the port when the Germans arrived. The *St Denis* was scuttled where she lay, but the *Malines* sailed after dark beneath the enemy's guns along the blacked-out channel. Aboard were 2,000 passengers plus the crew of the *St Denis*; all arrived safely at Tilbury the following morning.

The *Malines* later made further trips to Belgium when that country was overrun, and saved 1,000 men from the torpedoed destroyer HMS *Grafton* off Dunkerque. Finally, on 29th July 1942, the *Malines* was herself torpedoed and beached on the Egyptian coast near Port Said. She was raised the following year and used as a static training ship at Kabret. At the end of the war she was towed back to the Tyne, a journey that took six months, but repairs were never put in hand and the hulk was demolished in 1948.

The *Antwerp* survived the war alone, the *Bruges* being lost at Le Havre where she was bombed in June 1940. The *Antwerp* was headquarters ship for the invasion of Sicily in July 1943, and in 1945 she returned to Harwich as a troopship on the Hook of Holland route. Her last sailing was on 1st May 1950 from the Hook of Holland, and she lay for nearly a year at the buoys off Parkeston Quay before being sold for demolition. Of the early single reduction geared ships she was survived only by the *Hantonia*, and she too followed to the breakers yard only a few months later.

Table 2 : Single reduction geared turbine steamers planned or ordered before the Great War

	Owner	year built	scrapped /lost	tons (gross)	power+ (kilowatts)	speed (knots)
Hantonia	London & South Western Railway	1911	1952	1,560	3,700	19
Normannia	London & South Western Railway	1911	1940	1,567	3,700	19
King Orry	Isle of Man Steam Packet Company	1913	1940	1,877	7,000	21
Paris	London, Brighton & South Coast Railway	1913	1940	1,774	10,400	24
Biarritz	South Eastern & Chatham Railway	1914	1949	2,495		23
Maid of Orleans	South Eastern & Chatham Railway	1914	1944	2,384	7,500	23
St Seiriol*	Liverpool & North Wales Steamship Company	1914	1918	927		17
Lorina	London & South Western Railway	1918	1940	1,504	3,700	19
Curraghmore	London & North Western Railway	1919	1935	1,587		20
Anglia	London & North Western Railway	1920	1935	3,460	12,000	24
Antwerp	Great Eastern Railway	1920	1951	2,957		21
Bruges	Great Eastern Railway	1920	1948	2,949		21
Cambria	London & North Western Railway	1920	1949	3,445	12,000	24
Hibernia	London & North Western Railway	1920	1949	3,458	12,000	24
Scotia	London & North Western Railway	1920	1940	3,441	12,000	24
Malines	Great Eastern Railway	1921	1948	2,969	5,600	21

*excursion steamer   +shaft or indicated power

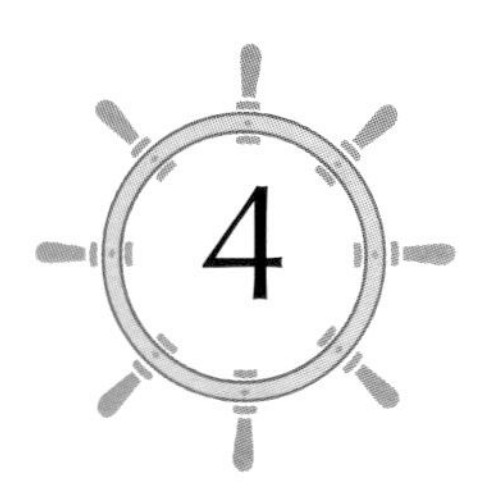

THE 'BIG FOUR'

The 1st January 1923 saw the grouping of the railway companies into the 'big four'. These were the Southern, Great Western, London, Midland & Scottish, and London & North Eastern Railways. The rationalisation of many of the services that followed was exemplified by the Holyhead to Greenore and Heysham to Belfast routes when the London & North Western and the Midland Railways both became part of the London, Midland & Scottish (see Chapter 3). It must also be remembered that the big four were to close a number of routes which would otherwise have suffered during the recession years of the 1930s.

Southern Railway

The first new tonnage to be delivered under the new grouping were the sisters *Dinard* and *St Briac*. They represented the first part of a massive rebuilding programme which the new Southern Railway had pledged at formation. However, there was considerable concern over the 1921 Railway Act, which had brought most of the independent railway companies into the four large groups, because rationalisation of the shipping services was inevitable. The Southern Railway was particularly vulnerable with four ports and five continental routes.

The first pair of new steamers came from the yard of William Denny in 1924, the *Dinard* launched on 2nd May and the *St Briac* on 2nd June. Invitations to tender for the construction of the ships were sent out on 7th September 1923 and the contract was awarded on 11th October. At that time, the Dumbarton yard had four river steamers for Paddy Henderson's Irrawaddy Flotilla on its books, a Nigerian Railways' train ferry, a passenger ferry for Brazil and a cargo passenger ship also for Hendersons.

The *Dinard* and *St Briac* each had two sets of single reduction geared turbines which generated a power of 3,900 kilowatts to maintain a service speed of 18 knots. The high and low pressure units were mounted side by side and drove a pinion on either side of the main gear wheel. The high pressure turbine included two rows of velocity compounded impulse blades, the remainder being of the reaction type. The low pressure ahead turbine blades were all of the reaction type, and at the forward end of the low pressure casing the reverse turbines had both impulse and reaction type blades. The turbine controls were on the lower manoeuvring platform and governors were fitted for emergency shut-off of steam.

The steam was supplied at 12 bar from two return tube marine boilers, one double ended, one single ended. The furnaces, each 6 m in diameter, could burn either coal or oil, and worked on the closed stokehold system. The oil bunkers were arranged either side of the single ended boiler, and the coal bunkers were situated alongside the double ended boiler. There was also two steam-driven generators to supply lighting and power plus two paraffin generators to pump and pre-heat the oil fuel, as well as to supply the galley and power the bilge pump when in port.

The ships had a gross tonnage of 2,291 when built, and were 99 m long by 12 m wide. They were the first cross-channel ships capable of burning oil fuel, and a premium of £7,100 was paid to the builder to adapt for both coal and oil burning during the building of the first ship; the pair otherwise cost £265,000. They were of riveted construction and the hull was subdivided by twelve transverse watertight bulkheads. The ships unusually also had a subdivided double bottom. There were eight 9 m wooden lifeboats stowed beneath Welin quadrant davits; two of the boats being aft abreast of the deckhouse which contained the second class smokeroom.

The *Dinard* and *St Briac* were designed for the overnight Southampton to St Malo service, which, until the St Malo Basin was completed in 1931, was timetabled according to tide. The ships could accommodate 850 first class and 450 second class passengers with berths for 324 first class and 118 second class. They each required a crew of 60. The first class dining saloon on the Main Deck provided for 60 at a time and was decorated in Jacobean style dark oak. A lounge panelled in light oak was situated at the forward end of the Boat Deck next to the first class entrance hall, and aft was a Jacobean first class smoking room and bar. There was a ladies' lounge at the after end of the Promenade Deck. Sleeping accommodation was provided in six 'cabins de luxe' plus 70 two berth cabins on the Promenade and Main Decks, as well as 80 more berths on the Lower Deck. Each cabin was decorated in silver-grey plane wood.

The second class sleeping accommodation was in six segregated ladies' and gents' open saloons at the after end of the Main Deck. One of these saloons also doubled as a dining saloon. There was also a smokeroom on the Boat Deck. In 1931, the second class accommodation was improved by replacing the canvas screen around the stern quarter with steel plating. The ships also had bow rudders fitted to assist handling in cross-winds.

In 1929 traffic on the St Malo and Channel Islands routes out of Southampton amounted to 1,500 return trips, carrying 266,400 passengers, 212,750 tons of cargo and an amazing 2,560 motor vehicles. However, in the 1930s, the *St Briac* made a considerable name for herself as a cruise ship. She was limited to an average of 165 passengers and even had a collapsible open-air swimming pool on the after deck. An initial series of weekend cruises out of Southampton commenced on 3rd June 1932 and was such a success that a total of 15 cruises were run that year. A further 22 cruises were operated in 1933 and in 1934 a total of 3,368 passengers enjoyed 19 cruises and these realised a profit of £2,752 for her owners.

During the war, both ships served as military transports and survived the Dunkerque evacuation. Thereafter, the *St Briac* was attached to the Fleet Air Arm training school at Arbroath, during which duty she was mined and sunk in March 1942 with the loss of 43 men. On 7th June 1943, the *Dinard* was badly damaged by a mine off Juno Beach but managed to return to Southampton for repairs, and was eventually able to recommence the Channel Islands service in July 1945. The following year, she was withdrawn from service and taken in hand by Palmer's Hebburn yard for conversion into a stern loading vehicle and passenger ferry. In this capacity her gross tonnage was reduced to 1,769, and she carried only 300 passengers along with 80 vehicles.

On 1st July 1947, the *Dinard* commenced service between Dover and Boulogne as a car ferry, where she replaced the crane loading car carrier *Autocarrier* which was then considered too small for the post-war service. The first season closed on 4th October, by which time the *Dinard* had carried 8,400 cars and 26,000 passengers. She continued in this service for ten years, commencing roll-on services at Boulogne in 1952, and at Dover in June 1953, as shore-side facilities became available. In the summer of 1952 she was sent over to Southampton each weekend to do a single Southampton to St Malo return; this was not repeated in subsequent summers as there was an average of only 27 cars on offer per voyage.

The *Dinard* worked alongside the *Lord Warden* for much of her career as a car ferry. Life was not without incident, and on 25th August 1956 she hit the Dover ramp with such force that she damaged her stern, injuring four passengers. Eventually, and at the great age of 34 years, she was displaced by the new steamer *Maid of Kent* (see Chapter 11). Nevertheless, she had another eleven years service under the Finnish flag with the name *Viking*.

In addition to revitalising the Southampton to St Malo route with replacement tonnage, the Southern Railway ordered new ships for the Dover station, and for the Newhaven to Dieppe service.

Isle of Thanet (1925) operated the Folkestone to Boulogne route in the post-war years. (FotoFlite)

The first of these were another pair, the *Isle of Thanet* and the *Maid of Kent* which were designed for the Dover Strait services. They were built by William Denny and equipped with double pairs of Parsons' turbines with steam provided by five Babcock and Wilcox boilers which were fired by oil. This gave them a speed of 22 knots. Of the two, the *Maid of Kent* was said to be superior.

The order for these two ships was precipitated by a favourable exchange rate with the franc throughout 1924 which had prompted considerable congestion on the route. Delivered in July and October 1925, they were big ships, capable of carrying 1,000 first class and 400 second class passengers in what was described as solid and comfortable accommodation rather than luxurious. There were six two-berth cabins on the Boat Deck, two singles for disabled people and two large deluxe cabins. There was a lounge on A Deck for 120 passengers, a saloon aft for a further 130, and amidships were 16 first class cabins. On the Main Deck was the restaurant which seated 96, a smoke room and lounge, and the second class dining saloon.

The *Maid of Kent* carried the future Duchess of Kent, Princess Marina of Greece, across the Channel to become Prince George's bride in 1934. Sadly, the ship was not to survive far into the war years and was lost in an air raid on Dieppe Harbour in May 1940; only 54 of the 90 people on board survived. The *Isle of Thanet* fared better in the war. Equipped as a hospital ship, she made three Dunkerque trips. Arriving first at 14.00 hours on 23rd May 1940, she had made it back as far as Dover by 23.00 hours to disembark 296 wounded men at Newhaven early the next morning. At 22.00 hours on 25th May she was back, and had moored alongside the *Canterbury* (see below) to load 600 wounded, returning to Newhaven at 08.30 hours on 26th May. By 04.30 hours on the 27th she was back off Dunkerque but was forced to return to sea against heavy shelling from the German batteries. Twelve hours later, she returned to be driven away again, returning empty handed after a minor collision in the black-out in the early hours of 28th May.

In July of that year she was sent to Preston as a submarine target ship and was later used at Dundee for exercises with the Fleet Air Arm. She became the Admiral's Headquarters ship for Force J landing troops in Normandy, oddly flying both an admiral's flag from the fore and the Red Ensign aft. At the end of the war she brought Polish refugees from Ostend, and then acted as a troopship between Newhaven and Dieppe. She returned to the Dover Strait in 1947 and inaugurated the post-war services out of the severely damaged port of Boulogne on 1st July, dressed overall.

Next spring the *Isle of Thanet* re-opened the Folkestone to Calais service after a Government ban on foreign travel had closed the service for the winter. Thereafter, she operated both Boulogne and Calais services until she was relegated to reserve ship in 1952. Nevertheless, every Friday for the next six summers she travelled light to Southampton to take an overnight relief service to Guernsey returning on Saturday morning, and back light again to Folkestone in time for a relief Boulogne service on Sundays.

The elderly ship was given a new lease of life in 1955, when no-passport day-trips were at last permitted to operate again to Continental ports. This gave her midweek employment which developed into three cheap-day-return trips per week by 1957 and, by 1960, she was fully employed on day trip work and weekend relief services. Although she had become a very expensive unit to maintain, her life was extended by a major overhaul. Her owners were reluctant to invest in new tonnage for the Dover Strait in case the much talked about Channel Tunnel would suddenly and miraculously appear out of the soil, on either side of the water, and take away their business.

The last day of service for the *Isle of Thanet* was 15th September 1963, a hot Sunday with a calm sea. She left Folkestone at 13.45 hours, again dressed overall, and now under the command of Captain Edgar Blaxland, the nephew of her very first master. She left Boulogne at 17.15 hours amid a crowd of onlookers and a noisy salute from the ships in port. By 18.45, she was alongside at Folkestone for the last time, having been in service for just over 38 years.

Southern Railway's next ship was the *Worthing*, also a product of William Denny, but this time designed for the Newhaven to Dieppe service. She was a powerful ship with a design speed of 24 knots to cope with the longer crossing. She had parallel sets of triple Parsons' turbines with four Yarrow boilers fired by oil which provided steam at 17 bar. The machinery provided a power of 11,000 kilowatts. She cost £171,680, of which two-thirds was provided by the French and the remainder by the Southern Railway, continuing the agreement set up in 1862, between the shipowners Maples & Morris of Shoreham and the Chemin du Fer de l'Ouest. She was launched on 3rd May 1928 and carried out her maiden voyage on 23rd August. With a crew of 57, she had accommodation for 580 first class, 327 second class and 133 third class passengers.

The *Worthing* quickly settled onto the route. Although she was the first order for just a single ship placed by Southern Railway, a modified partner was later ordered in December 1931. This was the *Brighton*, launched on 20th November 1932, which cost only £169,950 under the same funding and ownership agreement. She was a slightly larger ship but had a draft of only 3.4 m to allow her to relieve on Channel Islands services. She was the first of the fleet to be equipped with Welin over-frame davits which gave her a relatively uncluttered boat deck.

During the war, the *Brighton* was lost in the same bombing incident as the *Maid of Kent* whilst the two ambulance ships were alongside at Dieppe in May 1940. The *Worthing* took part at Dunkerque and in the Normandy landings and spent much of the war as a Fleet Air Arm target ship. She returned to the Newhaven-Dieppe route in 1946. Ultimately replaced by new tonnage in 1955, she was sold for further service under the

Worthing (1928), on the Newhaven to Dieppe service. Her powerful engines could maintain a speed of 24 knots. (FotoFlite)

Greek flag, but facing a major survey in 1965, was eventually demolished.

The *Canterbury* was the last of the ships to be built for the Southern Railway in the 1920s. This was a special ship, built for a special purpose. She was to provide the sea connection between Dover and Calais for a new prestigious first class train and sea service between London and Paris. The boat trains were respectively named 'Golden Arrow' and 'Fleche d'Or' and the planned journey time between the two capital cities was 6 hours and 35 minutes. The new ship was equipped with two pairs of twin stage Parsons' turbines with steam provided by four oil-fired Babcock & Wilcox boilers at 16 bar. She was a development of the *Isle of Thanet* but was broader in the beam by 0.5 m. Her forward well deck was designed for the carriage of passengers' motor cars and palletised mail bags. She was ordered from William Denny on 23rd February and launched on 13th December 1928 and had cost £220,000 to build.

The *Canterbury* arrived at Dover at the end of April 1929 ready for the inaugural Golden Arrow service on 15th May. She had luxury accommodation for only 400 passengers, and features included a Palm Court Tea Lounge. She sailed at 12.40 hours each day, only 20 minutes ahead of the normal mail boat, usually the *Maid of Kent*, but both ships operated to good loadings. She was designed for quick docking and undocking rather than outright speed, but could manage 23 knots. Within a month of the new service commencing, she was taken out of service with shaft trouble. This was not resolved until 24th June, and a series of stand-ins were arranged, with the *Maid of Kent* preferred over the other options, which included the old *Biarritz* and *Riviera* and the *Maid of Orleans*. Thereafter, the new ship was mechanically reliable.

The onset of the depression placed the

prestigious service in jeopardy and during the 1931/32 winter the *Canterbury* was refitted to accommodate 1,400 passengers with reserved first class accommodation for the Golden Arrow passengers. This work increased her gross tonnage from 2,912 to 3,071. She continued on her Dover to Calais route throughout the 1930s but was requisitioned on 6th September 1939 as a military transport.

In May 1940 her duties included Dover to the Hook of Holland with the Guards; a week later to Rotterdam to collect refugees, then Cherbourg for 1,000 refugees for Weymouth; then to Dover and on to Boulogne. The following day she took 570 troops to Calais to take part in the siege of that town, returning with wounded soldiers, refugees and prisoners of war. In the latter part of the month she took part in 'Operation Dynamo', making her first trip from Dunkerque at 18.50 hours on 25th May, two days before Dynamo officially began, with 1,246 men aboard. On the following day she uplifted 1,340 troops and sailed from Dunkerque overnight, but she found returning on the 28th difficult, and the passage took her over 12 hours. Once back in Dunkerque she loaded 457 troops and 140 wounded in only one hour. She was back on 30th May when, despite heavy bombing, she embarked 1,950 men between 14.00 and 17.00 hours. Bomb damage on the return journey was only rectified by 3rd June when the ship was again at Dunkerque, although she had to leave with only 459 French troops aboard, fearful of stranding on a falling tide. These exploits earned her master, Captain Charles Hancock, the award of the DSC.

Later in the year, she moved to Scotland to develop skills as a Landing Ship Infantry. She also acted as a feeder ship to the trans-Atlantic troop carriers, and brought the first contingent of American soldiers into Britain. She was then heavily involved in the Normandy landings and by December 1944 was back in the Dover Strait as a troop transport before being released in February 1946 for a major refit on the Tyne to prepare her again for civilian duties. During her time as a landing ship her decks had been reinforced with concrete, the four lounges stripped and fitted with hammocks, and all alcoves and cabins removed to make room for support pillars for the landing craft davits. On 15th April 1946 she reopened the Golden Arrow service, but was shortly displaced onto a new Folkestone to Calais service, before moving onto the Folkestone to Boulogne route where she remained for the next 17 years. During this period she became the first cross-Channel vessel to be equipped with radar.

The *Canterbury* eventually finished her career on 27th September 1964. Towards the end, a distinct tail vibration had begun to make itself felt and fuel oil consumption had risen to 9 tons per crossing. During much of 1965 she lay awaiting a buyer at Dover. As her colleagues adopted the new blue hull and red funnel, the *Canterbury* remained throughout in black hull livery with the standard buff funnel and black top. She was ultimately towed to a Belgian scrapyard on 29th July 1965.

Great Western Railway

The other railway groups of the 'big four' were also building new ships during the 1920s. The first pair of ships ordered by the Great Western Railway was the *St Julien* and the *St Helier* which were built by John Brown at a combined cost of £248,000. These ships were delivered in time for the 1925 summer season on the Weymouth to Channel Islands services. They were equipped with two sets of double Parsons turbines, with four single ended boilers which burned fuel oil, and the ships were capable of 18 knots. Originally built with two funnels, the after ones were removed in 1927 along with the after docking bridge. Removal of this top hamper reduced excessive rolling in cross winds The ships had a gross tonnage of only 1,885, yet could accommodate over 1,000 passengers.

In their early careers they both managed to ram the pier at St Helier. The following year they briefly deputised for the coal burners on the Fishguard to Rosslare route during the coal strike of 1926. For the next twelve years they carried out their duties on the Channel Islands run without incident. Both attended at Dunkerque, and between them they made 14 trips and carried nearly 22,000 men to

St Julien (1925), off Jersey in June 1960, her last year of service. (Kevin Le Scelleur)

safety including a small number of refugees. The ships then carried out the same work at St Malo and Cherbourg but were too late to be of assistance at Brest and La Pallice. They then moved to the Mediterranean, the *St Julien* as a Hospital Ship and the *St Helier* as a Landing Ship Infantry. They were involved in the invasion of Italy and the campaign at Salerno before returning home in time for the Normandy landings, where the *St Julien* was mined and had to be towed back to Southampton.

Following a major refit, the *St Helier* resumed her overnight service between Weymouth, Jersey and Guernsey on 15th June 1946, and was joined by her sister in November. They remained so employed for the next 15 years but were withdrawn in September 1960 having become too expensive to maintain. Both ships were then sold for demolition.

London, Midland & Scottish Railway

Replacements for the steamers *Antrim* and *Donegal* and the direct-drive turbine steamer *Londonderry* were ordered from William Denny at a price of £216,000 per vessel for the overnight Heysham to Belfast service. The ships were given traditional Fleetwood names although the Fleetwood to Belfast service was to be closed in 1929. They were named the *Duke of Lancaster, Duke of Argyll* and *Duke of Rothesay* and were launched on 22nd November 1927, 23rd January 1928 and 22nd March 1928, respectively. They had twin funnels with cowl tops, cruiser sterns, and were equipped with bow rudders to assist reversing up the long channel into Heysham. Their designed speed was 21 knots and they were coal fired. The passenger accommodation was excellent with berths provided for 400 saloon and 110 steerage passengers. The sleeping cabins were on the Promenade Deck and the Bridge Deck as well the Main (C) Deck and Lower (D) Deck. A total of 1,600 passengers and about 300 cattle could be carried.

Life was relatively uneventful on the service, at least for the *Duke of Argyll* and the *Duke of Rothesay*. The *Duke of Lancaster*, however, was seemingly accident prone: she ran down a fishing boat off the Isle of Man within one month of being delivered.

Duke of Argyll (1928), lying alongside the North Quay at Heysham. (Mike Walker collection)

Later the same year she suffered a minor stranding at Heysham and a few months later she ran into the *Duke of Rothesay* at Belfast causing minor damage. Then, in November 1931, she caught fire whilst alongside at Heysham and was scuttled, causing extensive damage to her accommodation. Once raised, repairs were put in hand by her builders at a cost of £108,000. However, back in service she later ran aground on Copeland Island in fog (June 1932); collided with a trawler near Heysham (1934); ran aground near the Point of Ayre on the Isle of Man (June 1937) and hit and sank the coastal collier *Fire King* in (January 1940). Rumour also had it that the *Duke of Lancaster* was haunted, the ghost being confined to the after part of the ship near the mortuary.

During the war the three ships served as Hospital Ships and Landing Ships Infantry. All three were involved in the Normandy Landings. During 1946 the sisters were reconditioned and returned to the Heysham to Belfast service. Replaced by ships of the same name (See Chapter 10) the *Duke of Lancaster* was towed to the breakers yard in October 1956, the *Duke of Rothesay* left in January 1957 and the *Duke of Argyll* departed the following summer.

London & North Eastern Railway

The last new buildings for the railways in the 1920s were the trio *Vienna, Amsterdam* and *Prague* for the Harwich to Hook of Holland service. They were built by John Brown and were equipped with two sets of twin Brown-Curtis turbines, each comprising one high and one low pressure turbine, and steam was provided by 5 single ended coal-burning boilers. They had a gross tonnage of 4,220 and were 107 m long with a beam of 15 m. They could accommodate 444 first class and 104 second class passengers, and there was space aft for the carriage of motor cars. The *Vienna* entered service on 15th July 1929, after being shown off to the public in Amsterdam on the 12th and Rotterdam on the 13th; her two sisters followed her into service early the following year.

During the 1930s, the *Vienna* carried out a

number of seasonal continental cruises. At the onset of war the ships adopted troopship duties, the *Amsterdam* and *Prague* later becoming a Landing Ship Infantry and a Hospital Ship respectively, in readiness for the Normandy Landings; the *Amsterdam* was mined and sunk off the beaches on 6th June 1944 with the loss of 33 men. The other two ships survived the war; the *Prague* returned to her civilian duties, but the *Vienna* was retained as a troopship operating to the continent out of Harwich and Tilbury. The *Prague* was returned to her builder in 1948 for a well deserved refurbishment. Alas, this was never completed as the ship was gutted by fire whilst at the shipyard where she was later declared a constructive total loss. The *Vienna* had been refitted to provide 1,048 berths for the troops. Her livery was grey hull with a broad blue band and yellow funnels. Although she had a boiler explosion in 1952 which killed two men, the old ship struggled on until she was finally withdrawn for demolition in 1960.

The *Vienna* was joined on the troop service by the oil engined *Empire Wansbeck*, which was laid down in 1939 but only completed in 1943 as the German *Linz*, and by the *Empire Parkeston*. The *Empire Parkeston* had originally been built by Cammell Laird in 1930 and was equipped with two sets of Parsons' triple expansion turbine engines with steam generated at 24 bar and 230°C by six Yarrow water tube boilers. These two ships had started their trooping careers between Harwich and Hook of Holland in 1947 and remained on the route until the continental trooping service was withdrawn completely in September 1961.

The *Empire Parkeston* started life as the *Prince Henry*, one of three sisters built by Cammell Laird in 1930 for the Vancouver based services of the Canadian National Railway. As built, the *Prince Henry* sported three funnels and had a gross tonnage of 6,893. She was elegantly fitted out to accommodate 400 first and second class passengers, or she could be used as a day excursion boat with a capacity for 1,500. On trials she managed 23 knots. In 1938 the *Prince Henry* passed to the Clark Steamship Company of Quebec and was converted for cruising under the new name *North Star*.

She was requisitioned in 1939 and converted into the Armed Merchant Cruiser HMCS *Prince Henry*. Later in the war, she was refitted as a Landing Ship Infantry, and it was in this guise that she attended the Normandy beaches along with her sister *Prince David*. Paid-off in London in 1945, she then had a stint as an accommodation ship in Germany before being brought to Southampton to be converted into a cross-Channel troop carrier, now with a gross tonnage of 5,556, and placed under the management of the General Steam Navigation Company.

There were three-tiered bunks for 813 troops in the rather bleak and gloomy troop decks. There was also accommodation for 182 passengers in cabins which could accommodate between two and eleven people; these were usually reserved for higher ranking men, for women and for families. Speed was reduced for economical reasons to a night crossing at 16 or 17 knots. In 1962, her service as a "leave boat" finally over, the former luxury Canadian steamer was sold for demolition.

EXCURSION SHIPS AND ESTUARINE FERRIES

A number of turbine excursion steamers and estuarine ferries were built between the two wars. The design of these steamers ranged from the experimental to the traditional. The geared turbine was now standard for fast light cross-channel steamers, and for the fast liner services, but it was also increasingly being adopted for many vessels which operated at slower speeds.

Short-sea passenger ships need to attain maximum speed in minimum time. An obvious development was to investigate the desirability of using higher steam pressures which could be generated with naval type boilers. Just as the original turbine steamer, the *King Edward*, had been built for demonstration purposes by a consortium of interested parties for service on the Clyde, so also was the *King George V*, which was put into service by Turbine Steamers Limited in 1926 (see Chapter 1).

King George V (1926), arriving at Oban from the round Mull and Iona excursion for David MacBrayne. (author)

The delivery pressure of 38 bar at 400°C was rarely exceeded in British short-sea vessels; the turbines of the *Holyhead Ferry I*, which was delivered in 1965 for service on the Irish Sea, were, for example, designed to use steam delivered at a pressure of 45 bar (Chapter 11).

The *King George V* was built with one quadruple expansion engine on the port shaft and two conventional triple expansion turbine units on the central and starboard shafts. The experiment ended when a water tube in the boiler burst, blowing off the furnace doors, filling the stokehold with fire and steam and killing two men. This incident happened at the end of her second season on the Clyde whilst the ship was approaching Irvine Harbour for winter lay-up. Fortunately, the collier *Prase* had just left Irvine before the excursion ship was disabled, and the collier managed to prevent the *King George V* from drifting ashore before the harbour tug was able to come to the rescue.

Happily, the *King George V* led a relatively uneventful life thereafter, being reboilered to provide steam at more conventional pressure that same winter and later having the extra high pressure turbine removed. Not only was the original machinery of the *King George V* experimental, but so too was her accommodation. Her Promenade Deck was partly enclosed and the dining saloon was situated on the Main Deck aft rather than on the Lower Deck. Originally a coal burner, she was converted for oil fuel in 1951, she received a mainmast in 1952 to comply with new lighting regulations and in 1958 she was equipped with radar. Two of her six lifeboats were replaced with life rafts in 1959 and her passenger accommodation was extensively refurbished during overhaul periods in the early 1960s.

The *King George V* is best remembered for her years at Oban: Monday, Tuesday, Thursday and Friday around Mull calling at Iona, Wednesday only to Iona from Fort William via Oban and the Sound of Mull, and Saturdays Oban to Tobermory. There were no Sunday sailings.

The year before the *King George V* entered service the *Glen Sannox* was commissioned by the London, Midland & Scottish Railway for the Ardrossan to Brodick service. Launched on 24th February 1925, she was built by William Denny at a cost of £58,500, and was almost a duplicate of the 1906 built *Duchess of Argyll*, with identical hull dimensions. This is possibly why she had three shafts, as in the original hull design, rather than two as would be expected in a single reduction geared ship; she had three single reduction geared turbines, one high pressure and two low pressure, driving the three separate propellers. Her design speed was 19 knots but she managed over 21 knots on trials and is reputed to have achieved 23 knots on occasion. She had a high design power for going astern, with the idea of slowing the ship on the approach to each terminal, so cutting the voyage time. This idea was not a success and was not repeated on Clyde steamers.

The *Glen Sannox* had a continuous Main Deck from the bows to just short of the stern, a centrally placed Boat Deck and two thin but well raked funnels. Her first class accommodation was forward and second class aft; she was licensed to carry 1,622 passengers on the Arran route and she required a crew of 35. In 1936 her ownership passed to the Caledonian Steam Packet Company when she began also to run on to Campbeltown after calling at Brodick; the *King George V*, which had been part of the Williamson Buchanan fleet, had then been transferred to Oban under MacBraynes. In the war, the *Glen Sannox* remained on the Clyde apart from a brief spell at Stranraer. She then continued on the Brodick service until the end of the 1953 season when she was displaced by a motor ship of the same name.

The old Williamson Buchanan steamer, *Queen Alexandra*, which dated from 1912, also became part of the MacBrayne fleet in 1936, and she emerged from winter lay-up resplendent in her new livery with the name *Saint Columba.* She had three new funnels which were slightly stepped, more oval and shorter than her old ones, and was placed on the Glasgow to Ardrishaig service leaving Glasgow Bridge Wharf daily at 07.10 hours. She was converted to oil burning in 1937, and remained on her long distance summer excursion route until withdrawn and scrapped in 1958.

Duchess of Hamilton (1932), at Rothesay in July 1967. (author)

The next pair of Clyde excursion steamers were built for the Caledonian Steam Packet Company on traditional lines with no innovation about them whatsoever. These were the *Duchess of Montrose* and the *Duchess of Hamilton*. The two ships were styled on the original *King Edward*, not only in design, but also the layout of the passenger accommodation and strangely also the machinery. They were built with triple screws to the same Edwardian direct-drive formula as *The Queen* and her consorts. Whether this was an act of conservatism by the board of the Caledonian Steam Packet Company or whether there was some ulterior motive for reversion to this acknowledged inferior system is unclear from the surviving literature. Nevertheless, the two ships were highly successful and extremely popular with the travelling public.

The *Duchess of Montrose* was launched from Denny's yard on 30th May 1930, at a cost of £76,800. She had a long Main Deck and centrally placed Promenade Deck with a teak bridge set back from the forward end of the superstructure. She was commissioned as a one-class ship, specifically for long-distance excursion traffic, and could carry 1,310 passengers on a Class 3 Certificate. She had a large observation lounge beneath the bridge, and there was a small lounge as well as the dining saloon on the Main Deck. Her traditional triple screw direct drive machinery was powered by steam at the then relatively low pressure of 12 bar, but the ship managed over 20 knots on trials. Her maiden commercial voyage was on 1st July, but mechanical failure made her return to Gourock before re-entering service a week later. Her main services before the war were the Kyles of Bute cruise, and the Ayr and Ailsa Craig excursions; she also operated on the Wemyss Bay to Rothesay ferry.

Her younger sister, the *Duchess of Hamilton*, came from the Govan yard of Harland & Wolff in 1932. The builder provided the direct-drive machinery which was constructed at Harland's Belfast yard, as well as the high speed propellers, which gave her ample capacity for 20 knots in her early years. Also commissioned as a one-class ship, the *Duchess of Hamilton* quickly established herself as the Ayr excursion steamer, although she also operated out of Troon and Ardrossan. During the war, she was used on the Stranraer to Larne crossing which had attained a significant military role in servicing the numerous training exercises that were carried out in Northern Ireland. In post-war years she was principally based at Gourock, with two weekly visits to Campbeltown, one to Inverary, one to Ayr and one to Arran via the Kyles of Bute with a cruise onwards to Pladda.

Memories of the ship are best summarised by this passage which first appeared in ***Paddle Wheels*** January 1972:

> *It was a Thursday early in September, and as I clambered up the steep gangway onto her Upper Deck I looked forward to one of those idyllic days, spent gliding silently over the Firth of Clyde, south past the heather-clad slopes of Arran to Campbeltown. Clattering down the wide staircases to the observation lounge or the Main Deck, and exploring the long passages to the engine room, a maze of pipes, gauges, catwalks, and polished brass, was a delight in itself.*

The anonymous report continues with a quote from Alan Paterson:

> *To stand at the engine room hatch and watch the ship cutting effortlessly through the glassy waters on a fine morning, with the steady hiss of the turbines and the noise of the auxiliary machinery the only sign of activity, was an unforgettable experience.*

The *Duchess of Montrose* carried out her final sailing on 30th August 1965 and left the Clyde later that week for a Belgian scrapyard. Her younger sister was withdrawn at the end of the 1970 season and scrapped four years later at Troon.

One more twin funnel, direct-drive turbine steamer with triple screws was yet to be commissioned. This was the *Queen Mary* which came from the William Denny yard in 1933 to the order of Williamson Buchanan Steamers. Outwardly, this coal-burning steamer looked like all her predecessors, but her passenger accommodation was designed afresh to a much more modern layout. She carried 1,524 passengers on summer cruises and was restricted to a certificate for 1,333 during winter duties. She was built as a two-class ship, with first class or cabin class forward, and second class aft. However, the Boat Deck was extended aft so allowing second class passengers access to the top deck, plus shelter below. She was also distinctive in that she had a solid bulwark to the bows instead of the normal handrail, and access to the Foredeck was via a stairway down from the Promenade Deck, rather than a doorway from the forward lounge. The first class dining saloon was below the Foredeck, and second class passengers had access to a tearoom, soda bar, smokeroom and bar.

The first master of the *Queen Mary* was Captain Donald McKinnon. The ship was placed on the Glasgow down-river service to Dunoon and Rothesay with the traditional departure time of 10.00 hours. The previous incumbent, the *King Edward*, was then relegated to the 11.00 hours departure for the Kyles of Bute. After only one year, her ownership was transferred to the Caledonian Steam Packet Company although it temporarily reverted to Williamson Buchanan Steamers (1936) until the war. She gave her prestigious royal name away to the Cunard Line in 1934, only losing the suffix II in 1976 when the famous trans-Atlantic liner *Queen Mary* was finally withdrawn from service.

During the war, the *Queen Mary II* stayed on the Clyde, and was later able to revert to her normal peace time duties without incident. She was converted to burn oil-fuel in 1957 when she received new water tube boilers. She also lost her two funnels and received a single large oval funnel. She was further modernised in 1971, when a new bar was built on the Boat Deck. The *Queen Mary* remained on the Glasgow down-the-river sailings to the end, her final sailing being on 27th September 1978. Eventually, she found her way, minus her engines, to a static role on the Embankment at London, where she is still used as a restaurant. In

Queen Mary II (1933), at Gourock in July 1969. The present day appearance of this ship is shown on the front cover. (author)

this guise she has been given back two funnels. As such, the *Queen Mary* is the last direct-drive turbine steamer in Britain. In 1992, the insured cost of ship and business was £2.5 million - her original cost to Williamson Buchanan Steamers in 1933 was a mere £61,805.

The last Clyde turbine steamer was the *Marchioness of Graham* which was built at a cost of £52,000 by the Fairfield Shipbuilding & Engineering Company at Govan for the Caledonian Steam Packet Company. She was launched on 6th March 1936 and on trials attained just under 18 knots. She had twin sets of turbines and conventional single reduction gears to two shafts. She was placed on the Ardrossan to Brodick service where she replaced the *Atalanta* (Chapter 2). The *Marchioness of Graham* stayed on the Clyde during the war. Returning to commercial service, she replaced the *Duchess of Hamilton* as the Ayr excursion steamer, except on summer Saturdays, when she reverted to the relief Arran steamer from Ardrossan. She was withdrawn in 1958, and was sold for further trading under the Greek flag. At this stage, she had her coal-burning boilers and turbine engines stripped out in favour of a motor engine and was also lengthened, later to be scrapped in 1981.

Only five turbine steamers were ever built for excursion services away from the Clyde. These were the direct-drive steamer *Kingfisher* of the General Steam Navigation Company (Chapter 2), the *St Seiriol*, built in 1914 for the Liverpool & North Wales Steamship Company, but lost in the Great War (Chapter 3), the steamers *St Tudno* and *St Seiriol*, built between the wars for the same company and, lastly, the *Empress Queen*, which was completed for P & A Campbell in 1940.

The Liverpool & North Wales Steamship Company had acquired the magnificent paddle steamer *La Marguerite* from the Thames operator New Palace Steamers in 1904. She had been built in

The GSNC Thames excursion steamer *Kingfisher* (1906) was based at Tilbury until sold in 1911.
(P&O Steam Navigation Company)

St Seiriol (1931) was a popular ship on North Wales and Isle of Man excursions. (Malcolm McRonald)

Empress Queen (1940), leaving Ryde Pier en route from Brighton to Bournemouth, in the summer of 1947.
(Richard Danielson collection)

1893, and was designed to carry out the daily Tilbury-Boulogne excursion at a service speed of 21 knots with a passenger complement of 3,000 in two classes. The Liverpool & North Wales Steamship Company had lost their brand-new turbine steamer *St Seiriol* in the Great War (Chapter 3) and had replaced her with the steam reciprocating engined *St Elian*, formally the Hamburg-Amerika Line tender *Hörnum*, which had originally been built as a German minesweeper. The *St Elian* remained in service until the 1927 season. A brand-new geared turbine steamer, the *St Tudno*, was launched from the yard of Fairfield Shipbuilding & Engineering on 2nd February 1926, and the *St Seiriol* followed in 1931.

The new *St Tudno* was 100 m long by 13 m giving her a length to breadth ratio of 7.5. Her gross tonnage was 2,326 and her design speed was 19 knots. She had twin sets of high and low pressure turbines with a power of 3,000 kilowatts, and which were connected via single reduction gears to twin shafts. There were two double-ended boilers which burned oil fuel under forced draught, and exhausted to a single raked funnel. She had a straight stem and a counter stern, and the Promenade Deck extended nearly the full length of the ship. She undertook her maiden voyage from Liverpool to Llandudno and Menai Bridge on 22nd May under the command of Captain W Highton.

The first season of the *St Tudno* was a difficult one. Although the ship was an oil-burner, the coal strike prevented train services from bringing passengers to Liverpool, and the company had to

St Tudno (1926) in the Mersey, waiting to come alongside Princes Landing Stage, ready for her morning departure to Llandudno. (John Shepherd collection)

resort to providing their own connecting bus services from major centres in Lancashire and elsewhere. Nevertheless, she soon proved a worthy successor to the *La Marguerite* and quickly became a favourite with the travelling public. A smaller sister, the *St Seiriol*, was built also by Fairfields and she undertook her maiden voyage to North Wales on 23rd May 1931. This ship had a gross tonnage of 1,586 and could accommodate 1,556 passengers in two classes. Her machinery (Figure 3) was similar to that of her sister although her design speed was slightly less. She provided sailings between Llandudno and the Isle of Man as well as feeder services between Liverpool and Llandudno.

Both ships were requisitioned during the war. The *St Tudno* was a depot ship in support of minesweepers and the *St Seiriol* was engaged initially as a tender on the Clyde and later as a troop transport between the Clyde and Northern Ireland. The *St Seiriol* distinguished herself under the command of Captain R D Dop at Dunkerque, where she came alongside the burning Thames paddler *Crested Eagle* to evacuate 150 troops.

Both ships were returned to Fairfields for extensive refurbishment and alteration at the end of the war. They emerged as one-class ships. The former second class dining saloon and café on the *St Tudno* became a large self-service cafeteria; the former first class smoke room became a soft drinks bar and the private cabins were reduced from five to three. There were two dining saloons on the Lower Deck with seating for 20 and 73 and there was a small saloon forward. The main dining saloon was on the Main Deck, along with a barber's shop and a lounge bar. On the Upper Deck was the main lounge, soft drinks bar and ladies' room. Here also was the Purser's office and a bar with access to the deck. The Upper Deck was characterised by large windows for which covers were available for use in inclement weather. Work carried out on the *St Seiriol* included the installation of central heating in all the public rooms as well as a self-service restaurant aft.

Both ships were back in service for the summer of 1946, the *St Seiriol* resuming commercial service with Captain Dop again in command. The schedule for the *St Tudno* was nearly always the same: 10.45 hours depart Liverpool, arriving at Llandudno at 13.05 hours and Menai Bridge at

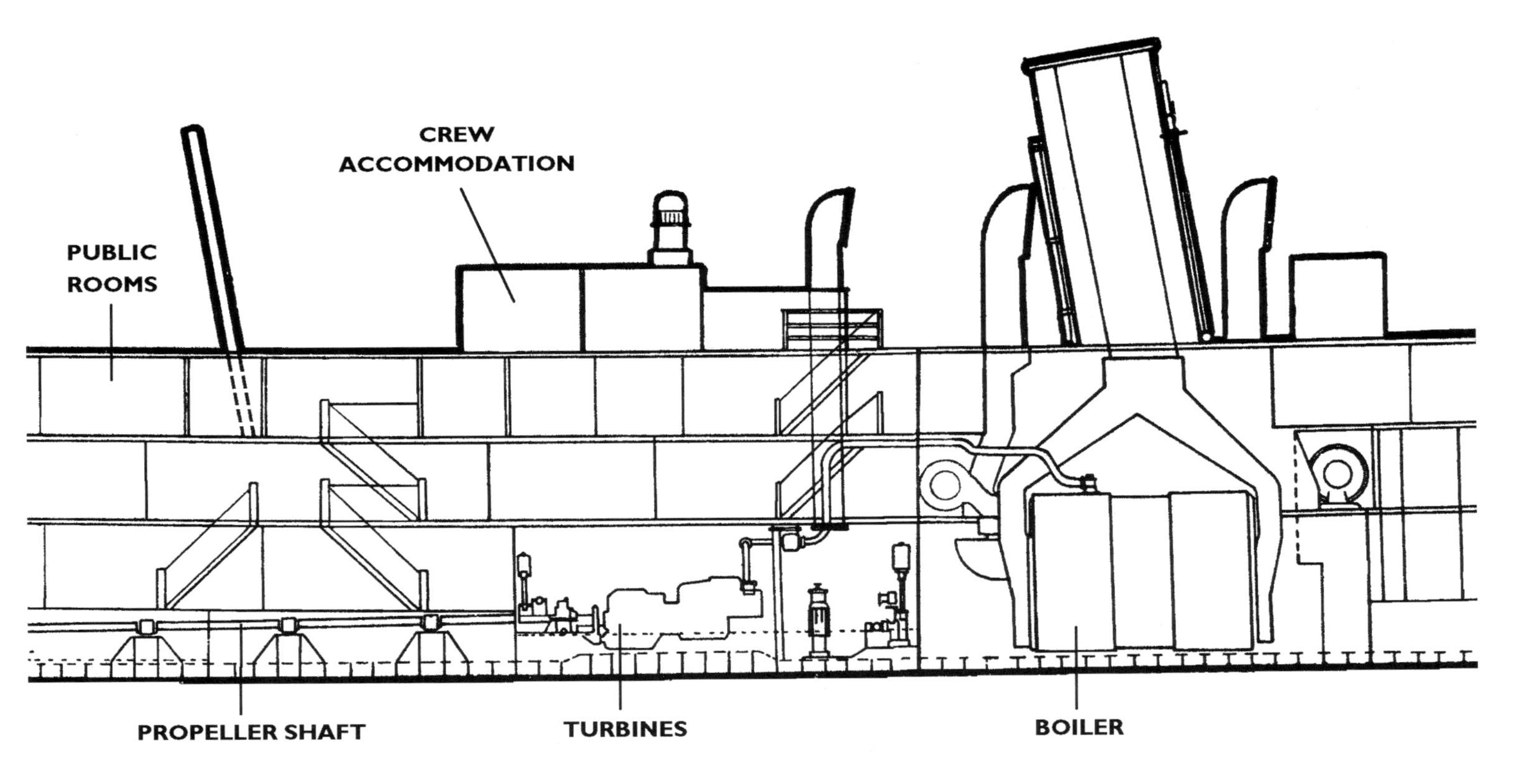

Figure 3 General machinery layout of the St Seiriol (1931).

14.35 hours. The return journey allowed a ten minute call at Llandudno with arrival at the Princes Landing Stage, Liverpool scheduled for 19.30 hours. Friday was her day off when the *St Seiriol* stepped in to the main line service. The smaller ship otherwise carried out 14.00 hour departures from Liverpool to Llandudno on Sundays, Mondays and Thursdays, 09.30 hours Thursday only from Llandudno to Liverpool and Tuesday and Wednesday returns from Llandudno to Douglas, Isle of Man.

The *St Seiriol* was withdrawn as an economy measure for the 1962 season, having made her last Douglas to Llandudno sailing on 6th September 1961. However, 1962 turned out to be the last year for the Liverpool & North Wales Steamship Company. Both steamers were then sold for demolition in Belgium, and a smaller diesel driven vessel, the *St Trillo*, was sold for further service with P & A Campbell.

The last turbine excursion steamer to be built was the *Empress Queen*, which was designed to augment the South Coast excursion services to France operated by P & A Campbell. She was built by the Ailsa Company at Troon with engines from Harland & Wolff at Belfast. The engines comprised conventional twin high pressure and low pressure turbine units connected via single reduction gears to two shafts. Her design speed was 21 knots and her gross tonnage was 1,781. She was launched on 29th February 1940 in wartime grey, and in December that year was converted to an anti-aircraft ship for use in the Thames and given the name *Queen Eagle*. She later undertook North Sea convoy escort duties and in December 1943 commenced trooping for the Ministry of War Transport between Stranraer and Larne.

Finally painted in civilian colours, the *Empress Queen* was prevented from taking up her no-passport excursion role in the post-war years as these services were not permitted to resume until 1955. In the meantime, the *Empress Queen* arrived at Bristol for the first time on 19th June 1947 following a major overhaul by her builders. She was tried on the Bristol Channel that month, but was found to be too big for many of the piers and even required tugs in the River Avon. She was then moved to Brighton to carry out coastal excursions which started on 7th July. She remained at Brighton for the next three seasons. In 1951 she ran from Torquay to Guernsey, Alderney and Bournemouth but was laid up at Bristol during the 1952 and 1953 seasons before being offered for sale. In April 1955 she left the Avon on eventual sale to Greek shipowners, ironically, in the same year that the day excursions to France were again permitted. Her new owners replaced her turbines with oil engines in 1959.

There was one other turbine excursion steamer under the British registry. This was the *Lady Enchantress* which was operated briefly out of Gravesend for the Three Star Shipping Company. She had been built in 1935 as the sloop *Bittern* and later became the Admiralty yacht *Enchantress*. She was bought from the Admiralty in 1946 for £22,500, but with conversion to a luxury day steamer her total cost rose to nearly £200,000. She started on the Gravesend to Margate run on 4th August 1947 in direct competition with the General Steam Navigation Company. Six weeks later, however, the economics of the venture required her withdrawal. She did not run again until 1950, when she had a brief and unsuccessful season out of Torquay which ended when the brickwork in her boiler collapsed.

CARGO AND CATTLE

Although the steam turbine engine had been widely adopted by the liner companies and the Admiralty, very few short sea cargo steamers were equipped with turbine engines. This was because service speeds did not warrant such equipment. The one exception was the Irish Sea services of the London, Midland and Scottish Railway for their overnight service between Dublin North Wall and Holyhead, and later for car capacity in support of the Heysham to Belfast mail ships. The Dublin cargo service was started in 1853, there being no cargo or cattle handling facilities at the mailboat terminal at Kingstown. Since the turn of the century, all the cargo ships were named after Irish Mountains (the Irish word Sliabh translates as Slieve).

In the late 1920s, the cargo fleet was rather dilapidated with only one new building in the previous 20 years. This was the *Slieve Donard* which had been built by Vickers at Barrow and whose twin four cylinder triple expansion engines gave her a speed of nearly 16 knots. She also had accommodation for 134 third class passengers, and it was this ship which always took the special Thursday daylight sailing from Dublin, known as the 'Kings of the Cattle Market'. which included a special three course luncheon on board. In 1929 a design for replacement ships was commissioned from William Denny and under this contract they delivered the *Slieve Bloom* in 1930 at a cost of £93,000. The ship had a well balanced profile with a single funnel with a cowled top (the cowl was later removed) and she had a cruiser stern. Gone were the traditional derricks, and in their place were electric cranes to speed up cargo handling operations. The ship had a gross tonnage of 1,297 and was 94 m long by 14 m beam.

The cattle decks were a vast improvement on the older ships, with stalls for 640 head of cattle and open deck space for sheep and pigs in pens which stowed away when not in use. The *Slieve Bloom* also had accommodation for twenty passengers. Other innovations included Brown hydro-electric steering gear, Columbus lifeboat davits and centrifugal windows on the bridge for clear sight. The biggest change of all was the propelling machinery: she was equipped with a pair of compound steam turbine engines with underslung condensers which were of very compact design to fit into the relatively small engine space. She had two Babcock and Wilcox coal-fired boilers which delivered steam at 16 bar. Her service speed was 16 knots. Like all the Dublin North Wall cargo ships she was registered at Dublin until 1939, and then re-registered at London. This was because until then, ships registered at Irish ports still flew the red ensign, but after the outbreak of war, neutral Ireland established a separate register under the Irish flag.

The new ship was such a success that a near sister was ordered from the same builders. The *Slieve More* was delivered in 1932, and although built to the same hull design, had a slightly larger gross tonnage of 1,370 because she had more extensive third class passenger accommodation with 20 berths and a certificate for 75 passengers including the cattle drovers. She had cost £88,224 to build. She also had a flying bridge, the result of two years operational experience with her older sister, but there was no cowl on her funnel. Although her machinery was the same as her sister's, she managed over 17 knots on trials and was then the fastest cross-channel cargo ship afloat.

By 1933, four of the older units of the fleet had been withdrawn, so efficient were the two newcomers. In 1935, William Denny delivered a third vessel to the same basic hull dimensions and gross tonnage as the *Slieve Bloom*, but with more

Slieve More (1932), the second of the cargo and cattle ships, alongside at Holyhead. (Malcolm McRonald)

powerful turbines which enabled a service speed of 17 knots. This was the *Slieve League*, and she was followed by an identical sister, the *Slieve Bawn*, early in 1937, and, a variation on the theme, the *Slieve Bearnagh*, in 1936. This trio had open alleyways along the sides of the superstructure with the lifeboats on the Bridge Deck. The *Slieve Bearnagh* was built for service between Heysham and Belfast and only rarely ran on the Holyhead to Dublin route, and then not until the 1950s and 1960s. With the arrival of the *Slieve League* and *Slieve Bawn* on the Holyhead service, all the non-turbine ships save for the *Slieve Donard* were withdrawn. All six ships remained in railway service on the Irish Sea throughout the war and returned to their peacetime duties once more on the Holyhead to Dublin and Heysham to Belfast route but minus their passenger accommodation.

The *Slieve Bearnagh* was the odd man out. She was built for the carriage of cars rather than just cattle and general cargo, and was never equipped with cranes or passenger accommodation. The need for a car carrier on the Heysham to Belfast route came about when the existing mail ships were converted for increased passenger accommodation at the expense of space for vehicles. The *Slieve Bearnagh* was specifically designed to run alongside the new *Duke of York* (Chapter 7) and was always registered at Lancaster. Interestingly, she was designed for port side loading only, and could accommodate 735 head of cattle and 14 horses. For the long stern-first approach to Heysham Harbour, she had an astern turbine which was capable of 70% of the power of the forward turbines. She also had shelters on the bridge wings to facilitate navigating the long channel up to Heysham. She had cost £91,725 to build.

All five turbine ships were coal burning. The *Slieve Bearnagh* and the *Slieve Bawn* were converted to oil, in 1960 and 1961 respectively, when modernisation of the crew's accommodation was also carried out. The other three ships and the *Slieve Donard* were coal burners throughout their careers.

The biggest change to affect the turbine ships was the introduction of the container, initially closed containers for perishable goods, which were introduced by the British Transport Commission after its formation in 1948. The early containers had a capacity of between 15 and 22 cubic metres and these could be transferred directly onto special rail wagons.

Slieve Bawn (1936), at the Holyhead Cargo Terminal in August 1966. (author)

Slieve Bearnagh (1936), arriving at Heysham, with *St David* on the Lay-by Berth, August 1970. (author)

During the 1950s, 7 ton cranes were installed at Dublin and Holyhead and the mainmasts of the ships were removed, but later restepped immediately forward of the funnel to provide a clear unobstructed after deck. The efficiency offered by partial containerisation eventually displaced the *Slieve Bawn* to Heysham to allow a nightly cargo service to Belfast, and saw the elderly *Slieve Donard* withdrawn for demolition during 1954.

A new motor ship with the name *Slieve Donard* came into service at Holyhead in 1959. Thereafter, the *Slieve Bloom* and *Slieve More* were increasingly laid up at anchor in the Outer Harbour at Holyhead. Eventually, in 1965, these two fine steamers were towed away to the breakers yard. The *Slieve League* followed in 1967, realising a seemingly small sale price of £14,000. At this time, the *Slieve Bawn* was returned briefly to the Holyhead service. By now the early experiments with small containers had led to the international standard container. The first of the new size containers was shipped on the Holyhead route in 1968, using the converted cargo ships *Harrogate* and *Selby* which had been displaced from the fleet of Associated Humber Lines. At Heysham, the purpose built *Container Enterprise* and *Container Venturer* had been handling the standard 'B' type railway container since 1958, and were later adapted for carriage of the international standard container.

The remaining turbine steamers, the *Slieve Bawn* and *Slieve Bearnagh*, were increasingly outmoded. However, they remained in service at Heysham, and carried out their final sailings before Christmas in December 1971, after which the carriage of live cattle ceased. As the *Slieve Bearnagh* sailed to lay up at Holyhead, speed was increased to a full 17 knots, the engines reportedly as good as new. The two ships were eventually sold for demolition in Spain after being twice resold by other scrapyards.

A number of other ships used a combination turbine and reciprocating engine. This used an early hybrid development using the combination steam reciprocating engine exhausting to a single low pressure turbine and first introduced in the New Zealand Shipping Company's *Otaki* in 1908. She had the turbine on the central shaft and two reciprocating engines on the wings. This arrangement allowed most of the remaining 0.5 bar of the steam above condenser pressure to be exhausted on the low pressure turbines. The White Star Line's *Olympic* and *Britannic* were equipped with the same machinery in 1911 and 1914 respectively. In post-war years the Bauer Wach system evolved which allowed the low pressure turbine to be on the same shaft as the reciprocating engine. This arrangement was designed specifically for tramp steamers and was widely used throughout the inter-war years.

After the Second World War, the Bauer Wach system became popular on the longer 'short sea' routes, not least in the North Sea and the Baltic. One of the main operators of this type of machinery was the Ellerman's Wilson Line (Table 3), which maintained a network of North Sea services with their distinctively coloured 'green parrots', small cargo ships which generally had accommodation for twelve passengers, and which had dark green hulls that complemented black-topped crimson funnels. Typical of these ships was the *Malmo* and her eight sisters which came from the West Hartlepool yard of William Gray & Company in the years immediately following World War II. This shipyard specialised in the Bauer Wach system, except that the low pressure turbine was connected through double reduction gears and hydraulic coupling. These ships were used on a variety of Scandinavian services out of the Humber, and were gradually withdrawn in the mid-1960s.

The *Borodino* was perhaps the ultimate in this design: completed in 1950 by the Ailsa Shipbuilding Company at Troon, she was also equipped with a triple expansion steam engine and a low pressure turbine with double reduction gearing and hydraulic coupling. This arrangement gave her a service speed of just over 13 knots. She had comfortable accommodation for 36 passengers and served almost her entire career on the Hull to Copenhagen route. She was not a big ship, with a gross tonnage of only 3,206. She was withdrawn prematurely after only 17 years service, her machinery being obsolescent from the start, and her service overtaken by the large capacity passenger and vehicle ferries on the Harwich to Esbjerg route.

The company continued to build ships with combination steam machinery until the mid-1950s. The last pair of ships was the *Cicero* and *Rollo*, which had a gross tonnage of 2,499 and which could maintain 13 knots. They were built by Henry Robb at Leith in 1954 for the Scandinavian services but ended their days on the Mediterranean routes to Greek and Turkish ports before being sold on for further service in 1970. The last of the fleet to be equipped with combination steam machinery was the *Teano*, completed in 1955. It is interesting to note that the company had introduced two diesel ships in 1951, but had otherwise shown a clear preference for the steam reciprocating and low pressure turbine system in rebuilding their fleet in the post-war years. The last of the passenger carrying steamers to be withdrawn were the *Volo* and *Truro* in 1968.

Other operators of the combination machinery included many of the liner companies: Brocklebank, Head, Charles Hill, Palm and Strick as well as most of the charter companies such as 'Hungry' Hogarth, Hain, France Fenwick and so on.

Table : 3 Ellerman's Wilson Line fleet list as at January 1960

Ship	Built	Tons gross	Engines
Albano	1947	2,239	turbine combination
Angelo	1940	2,199	turbine combination
Ariosto	1946	2,208	turbine combination
Borodino	1950	3,206	turbine combination
Bravo	1947	1,798	turbine combination
Carlo	1947	1,799	turbine combination
Cattaro	1945	2,890	steam reciprocating
Cavallo	1951	2,340	diesel
Cicero	1954	2,497	turbine combination
Dago	1947	2,302	turbine combination
Domino	1947	2,302	turbine combination
Electro	1937	793	diesel (aft)
Leo	1947	1,792	turbine combination
Livorno	1946	2,957	steam reciprocating
Malmo	1946	1,799	turbine combination
Palermo	1928	2,838	steam reciprocating
Rinaldo	1946	2,957	steam reciprocating
Rollo	1954	2,499	turbine combination
Silvio	1947	1,798	turbine combination
Spero	1922	1,580	steam reciprocating
Tasso	1945	1,648	turbine combination
Teano	1955	1,580	turbine combination
Tinto	1947	1,795	turbine combination
Trentino	1952	2,340	diesel
Truro	1947	1,797	turbine combination
Vasco	1939	2,829	steam reciprocating
Volo	1946	1,797	turbine combination

Passenger routes were Hull to Oslo, Copenhagen, Gothenburg and Stockholm; London to Oslo, Stockholm, Copenhagen, Gefle and Norrkoping; and Liverpool and Manchester to Stockholm. The cargo services were more widespread: from the Humber ports, Middlesbrough, London, Bristol Channel, Liverpool and Manchester to Scandinavian and other Baltic ports, as well as to Portugal, Spain, the Mediterranean, Black Sea, Red Sea and the Persian Gulf.

HEYDAYS - TO THE ISLE OF MAN AND THE CHANNEL ISLES

Ben-my-Chree (1927), seen leaving Douglas in 1965, her final year of service. (author)

The Isle of Man Steam Packet Company built three turbine steamers before the Great War: the direct-drive *Viking*, the fast and luxuriously appointed direct-drive steamer *Ben-my-Chree* which had been lost in the war, and the single reduction geared turbine steamer *King Orry*. In the immediate post-war years the company found itself under-capitalised and carried out a programme of buying up second-hand tonnage. This included the turbine steamers *Manxman*, formerly of the Midland Railway; the South Eastern & Chatham Railway steamer *Onward*, which was renamed *Mona's Isle*; G & J Burns' *Viper*, which became the *Snaefell*; and the London & South Western Railway's *Caesarea*, which became the *Manx Maid*. At a later stage, in 1928, the company bought the *Victoria*, a sister of the *Onward*, which entered the fleet without change of name, along with two elderly piston engined steamers from the London, Midland & Scottish Railway.

This influx of ships enabled the Isle of Man Steam Packet Company to get back on its feet and satisfy the massive post-war demand for holiday travel to and from the island. By the mid-1920s the company finally had enough funds to place an order for a new turbine steamer to be built to its own design. A contract was placed with Cammell Laird for £185,000, but work was delayed by the coal strike and the keel was not laid until November 1926. With the help of imported steel from the Continent, the ship was launched on 5th April 1927 and given the name *Ben-my-Chree.* The builders had made a substantial loss on the contract and it was later agreed that the company pay a final sum of £200,000 for the ship, which had also included a number of additions over and above the original contract.

The new *Ben-my-Chree* was a fine successor to her former namesake (Chapter 2). She had a gross tonnage of 2,586. Her twin turbine units could maintain a service speed of 21 knots, although she managed 24 knots on occasion. Her boilers were oil-fired, typically burning about 19 tons of oil on the run from Liverpool to Douglas. She had a tall funnel and sported five lifeboats either side, and the bridge was level with the Boat Deck. The stem was straight and she had a fine counter stern.

There was accommodation for 2,586 passengers in two classes. The public rooms were on three decks, with the Upper and Main Decks partially enclosed. Although she was commissioned with the usual black hull she was painted all white, with green boot topping, in the winter of 1931/2. This was a decision of the Board who decided that this livery would have a distinct advertising value whilst the ship was in the Mersey. It also coincided with a possible charter by the Roman Catholic church for a sailing to Dublin, in connection with the Eucharistic Conference of 1932, and Merseyside rumour had it that this was the real reason for the repaint even though the charter never actually took place because of her lack of overnight accommodation.

A bigger and grander version of the same design

Lady of Mann (1930), approaches the Princes Landing Stage at Liverpool in September 1968. (author)

followed in 1930, when the *Lady of Mann* was launched by the Duchess of Atholl, the Lady of Mann, on 4th March 1930. The ship was built by Vickers Armstrong at Barrow and cost £249,000. She was the largest ship ever built for the company and had a gross tonnage of 3,104, and a passenger capacity of 2,873. She was often referred to as the Centenary Ship, the Manx company having been founded in 1830. Her general arrangement was similar to that of the *Ben-my-Chree*, the main outward difference being that the bridge was placed above the Boat Deck. Her owners described her at the time as being 'foreman built', the depression having seen all but the foremen laid off from the shipyard. On delivery, she was placed on the Fleetwood to Douglas route. The *Lady of Mann* was delivered with the traditional black hull but this was soon changed to white and green.

During the war years, both ships were involved in the Dunkerque evacuation and were later involved in the D-Day Landings. They spent much of the rest of the war, trooping; the *Lady of Mann* having carried some 2 million troops. Both ships were extensively refitted at the end of the war and were able to resume civilian duties in 1946, resplendent with black hulls, red boot topping and a white line. The ships were little changed in appearance, but the funnel of the *Ben-my-Chree* was shortened in 1947, and the cowl removed in 1951, giving her a squat, but perhaps more up-to-date outline.

The two ships provided seasonal support in post-war years with their high passenger capacities. They were popular ships with the public and with the crews. Interviewed in 1969, Commodore Lyndhurst Callow, Captain of the *Lady of Mann*, described his favourite ship the *Ben-my-Chree* as 'a fine ship - she was kind to her master'. The *Ben-my-Chree* had been sold for breaking up at the end of 1965. Her last voyage from Douglas was the 00.01 hours departure on 13th September, leaving harbour with three short blasts on her siren and heading out into a warm windless night on course for Liverpool. The *Lady of Mann* lasted until August 1971 when she too went to the breaker's yard. In her final season she was allowed, on occasion, to run flat out. She could still maintain 23 knots with ease.

Three further Isle of Man boats were built during the 1930s, but all of these were lost in the war. These were the *Mona's Queen*, delivered by Cammell Laird in 1934, and the *Fenella* and *Tynwald* which were built together by Vickers Armstrong and both launched on 16th December 1936. The *Mona's Queen* was built much along the lines of the *Ben-my-Chree*. The main differences were that the new ship's bridge was placed right at the front of the superstructure giving her a blocky appearance, her fore deck was built one deck higher making her difficult to handle, and she had a less pronounced counter stern. Mechanically, she was the same, but she was the first ship of the Manx fleet to have water tube boilers rather than Scotch boilers which require more space. She was equipped with a bow rudder and had the new Oertz type of rudder aft. Furthermore, the company had now settled on a fleet running speed of 21 knots, now that the days of competition were over.

The *Mona's Queen* was launched in the new white and green hull colours. She had a certificate to carry 2,486 passengers and required a crew of 83. Her passenger accommodation included all the traditional public rooms, but she also had twenty private cabins which could be pre-booked. Sadly, the ship only enjoyed a few years in service. She was principally employed between Liverpool and Douglas and inaugurated the evening cruises from Douglas to the Calf of Man. Requisitioned as war was declared, she was mined off Dunkerque on 29th May 1940. This was her second trip into Dunkerque; the ship sank in only two minutes and 24 of her crew died, although the remainder of the crew were picked up by a destroyer.

The sisters, *Fenella* and *Tynwald*, were built to an entirely new design. They were intended for year round service and as such had a passenger capacity of only 1,968. The ships had a rounded and streamlined front to their superstructure, which was stepped to the open Main Deck aft where cars could be accommodated. They had squat flat topped funnels with cowls and were the first ships of the fleet to be built with cruiser sterns. Their design was so successful that a further six quasi-sisters were

The pre-war *Tynwald* (1937) had a more attractive paint scheme than her sister *Fenella.* (John Shepherd collection)

Fenella (1937), seen approaching Douglas during her all too brief civilian career. (John Shepherd collection)

later to be built after the war, the last of the series being the *Manxman* which was commissioned in 1955 (Chapter 10).

The *Fenella* and *Tynwald* cost £407,000 to build. They had a gross tonnage of 2,376, and both ships achieved well over 21 knots on trials; neither had bow rudders. Their twin turbines maintained a propeller speed of 275 revolutions per minute at 21 knots. The ships were launched with black hulls, the *Tynwald* being distinguished with a white upper strake, and both had the three legs of Man on their bows. During their short civilian careers they were mainly deployed on the Liverpool to Douglas route and were much appreciated by the travelling public, particularly during the winter months. The *Fenella* was also used to popularise low cost day excursions to Dublin and Belfast, and the *Tynwald* was used for similar excursions to Ardrossan during the British Empire Exhibition in 1938 at Bellahouston Park, Glasgow, and in 1939 had the honour of landing the first excursionists on the island on a Sunday.

The *Fenella* was sunk by a bombing attack whilst alongside at Dunkerque. She settled on the bottom astern of the burning Thames paddler *Crested Eagle*, as the *St Seiriol* lay off and rendered assistance with her boats. The *Fenella* had already embarked 650 men and most of them were able to scramble onto the pier, but 15 of the crew died. One of the crew was taken prisoner, but he survived the war even though he suffered severe burns in the incident. The ship was later broken up where she lay. The *Tynwald* managed to repatriate a total of nearly 9,000 troops in four separate trips to Dunkerque. Later in the year she was requisitioned and converted with the removal of her entire superstructure into an auxiliary anti-aircraft ship for coastal convoy escort duties. She was then sent south as part of the Allied Forces' landing on North Africa but was lost off Algiers on 12th November 1941.

The spate of new-building for the railways, which had started after the grouping of the 'big four', continued into the early 1930's and then came to an abrupt halt. Like the Isle of Man boats, all were built as twin screw single reduction geared turbine steamers. Some of the last cross-channel ships to be built with twin funnels were the sisters *Isle of Jersey* and *Isle of Guernsey*. They were products of William Denny and were launched on 22nd October and 17th December 1929 respectively. Like most ships then designed for the Channel Islands services they were flat bottomed so they could rest on the bottom at low tide. They entered service for the Southern Railway between Southampton, Jersey and Guernsey, and St Malo during March 1930. Their design speed was just over 19 knots; they were oil fuelled and had three single ended boilers and two pairs of turbines. Together the pair cost £340,000 to build.

The two 'Isles' were not big ships, with a gross tonnage of only 2,143. The passenger accommodation was of a high order, in two classes. For day sailings, up to 1,400 passengers could be seated and fed, and for night sailings (and short sea cruises) there were 154 first class berths. Their success in service led to the order of a third sister, the *Isle of Sark*. However, shortly after the keel was laid the hull shape and machinery were changed. The *Isle of Sark* was launched on 21st November 1932, complete with a cut-back Maierform bow, the first cross-Channel ship to be so equipped. She commenced on the overnight Southampton to Channel Islands service on 19th March 1932. The Channel Islands service became extremely popular during the 1930s and this is when the *Isle of Thanet* used to be drafted in from Folkestone to assist during summer weekends (see Chapter 4).

In December 1934 the Southern Railway was invited by Denny to install a prototype ship stabiliser system to one of their ships. The price was £4,400 and the cost of installation a further £2,800. It was agreed that Denny would pay a third of the total cost, unless the experiment failed, when they would carry two-thirds of the cost. In the event, the *Isle of Sark* was fitted with the prototype Denny Brown stabilisers at Southampton in March 1936. During trials the equipment was used to produce a 20° roll and shortly after she re-entered service a 10° roll was reduced to 5°. The stabilisers were particularly attractive on the Channel Islands service where much of the voyage can be spent broadside on to the Atlantic rollers. Six months

Isle of Guernsey (1930), seen off Jersey in August 1960, from the photographer's dinghy. (Kevin Le Scelleur)

Isle of Jersey (1930) was essentially similar in appearance to her sister (above). (Kevin Le Scelleur collection)

Isle of Sark (1932). Note the cut-back shape of the Maierform bow. (Malcolm McRonald)

later the Southern Railway duly paid its two-thirds share of the cost.

All three ships served with distinction during the war. The *Isle of Jersey* made eleven trips to the Normandy beaches as a Hospital Ship bringing some 2,000 injured men back to safety. The *Isle of Guernsey* was also converted as a Hospital Ship and she attended at Dunkerque bringing away over 800 injured; she became a Landing Ship Infantry for the D Day invasion and was the first ship to enter Arromanches. The *Isle of Sark* was the last ship to leave Guernsey on 28th June 1940 prior to the German invasion. She later became an auxiliary radar training ship. All three ships returned to civilian duties during 1946.

In 1948 the Southern Railway fleet passed to the British Transport Commission. The Channel Islands services continued in popularity but no effort was made to update the ageing fleet or to provide new tonnage. The three Isles soldiered on, no longer the last word in passenger transport, when finally the decision was taken to close the Southampton service. The *Isle of Guernsey* carried out the last sailing on 13th May 1961 and was sold for demolition later that year. The other two ships had been withdrawn the previous year, the *Isle of Sark* going to the breakers and the *Isle of Jersey* going to Libya for use as a pilgrim ship until she too went to the breakers in 1963.

Denny produced a fourth ship for the Southern Railway in 1933. This was the small steamer *Brittany*, of 1,445 tons gross and which was built for the Jersey to France routes. Outwardly, she appeared as a scaled down version of the Isles but with a single funnel. Her shallow draft of only 3 metres allowed her access to the port of St Malo at all stages of the tide, and she was designed to sit on the mud at St Helier. She was equipped with two pairs of turbines which were supplied by steam from an oil-fired Yarrow boiler, although there was also a small Scotch boiler for harbour use. Her service speed was 16 knots. She was launched on 12th April 1933 and cost £81,500 to build. Her passenger accommodation was on two decks, with capacity for 500 first class and 350 second class.

At the outbreak of war, the *Brittany* spent three

Brittany (1933) leaving St Helier, Jersey, on passage to St Malo. (Malcolm McRonald)

days on a shuttle service bringing holiday makers out of France to Jersey to connect with the steamer to Southampton. She then transferred to the Folkestone to Boulogne service, and was also present at Dunkerque. In September 1940 she was requisitioned as an auxiliary net layer for boom defences and then took up a variety of jobs which took her to the Eastern Mediterranean, India and the Seychelles. She was able to return to her service out of Jersey in 1946, where she continued for the next 16 years. During this period, she was also used for trips to Sark, as well as her ferry duties from Jersey to St Malo and Granville, and from Guernsey to Alderney, St Malo and Cherbourg. She had never been a profitable ship and she was finally withdrawn 'for reasons of economy' towards the end of the 1962 season when her duties were carried out on a reduced frequency by the *St Patrick* (see Chapter 9). After being laid up at Southampton for six months, the *Brittany* was sold for further service in the Baltic and converted into a roll-on car ferry. She was still capable of 16 knots, but she was finally broken up in 1972.

The Great Western Railway also put a new ship on the Channel Islands service from Weymouth, under the ownership of the Fishguard & Rosslare Railways and Harbours Company. She was the *St Patrick*, launched on the 15th January 1930 from the yard of Alexander Stephen & Sons at Glasgow. She was equipped with the normal arrangement of turbines with steam generated in four single ended boilers to a pressure of 16 bar. Her design service speed was 22 knots. She could accommodate 913 passengers in two classes, and had berths for 216 first class and with second class lounges set aside for men and women for night crossings. She was built as a replacement of the direct-drive turbine steamer of the same name (see Chapter 2), which was destroyed by fire alongside at Fishguard in April 1929. Although she was intended for duty at both Weymouth and Fishguard she spent most of her career on the Channel Islands service.

The *St Patrick* was designed along the lines of the *St Helier* and *St Julien* which the Great Western Railway had put into service on the Channel Islands service in 1925 (Chapter 4). Although the *St*

Patrick incorporated a number of modifications, the main differences were that she was designed as a single-funnelled ship and the funnel was therefore larger, while the forward well deck was plated over giving the ship a more modern appearance. Disaster struck on 5th August 1932 when the ship hit rocks off the Corbiere Lighthouse on Jersey. The ship was badly holed and her 314 passengers were transferred where she lay to the *Isle of Sark*. She was later taken into St Helier and on to Birkenhead for repairs costing some £2,000.

During the war, the *St Patrick* was left on the Fishguard to Rosslare service after an initial brief spell as a troop carrier. In August 1940, and again in May 1941, she was attacked from the air but on both occasions she was able to escape unhurt. In the early hours of Friday 13th June 1941 she was again attacked whilst on passage to Fishguard, about 22 km short of her destination. A stick of four bombs struck the cross-bunker fuel tanks which ran the breadth of the ship forward of the funnel, causing a terrific explosion. Critically hit, and with a broken back, the *St Patrick* sank in only seven minutes; 29 passengers and crew died, 60 survived, and with only one serviceable lifeboat, many survivors were in the water for up to 2 hours before help arrived.

The ship's pennant was later washed ashore and recovered. On 20th May 1947 the namesake and successor to the *St Patrick* was launched with the same battered pennant flying proudly from her masthead (Chapter 9).

The Isle of Jersey

Ordered from Denny on 31st January 1929, the *Isle of Jersey*, one of two sisters, was delivered six weeks early on 19th January 1930 at a cost of £170,271. She was built as a direct replacement for the *Alberta*, a triple expansion piston-engined ship built in 1900. The new *Isle of Jersey* was 93 m long by 13 m broad and had a draft of only 4 m. On trials she attained over 19 knots at 250 revolutions per minute. The ship's owners, the Southern Railway, commended her builders for designing a cross-Channel steamer for passengers who demanded "the luxury of a Savoy Hotel, the accommodation of a New York skyscraper, the steadiness of a transatlantic liner, and the speed of a torpedo-boat destroyer – all for the price of a ride in a London taxicab".

The *Isle of Jersey* was designed on two continuous decks: a Main Deck and a Promenade Deck. Watertight subdivision of the hull was achieved with twelve transverse bulkheads, and there was a subdivided double bottom along the full length of the ship. This provided considerable ability to withstand damage, and the double bottom tank provided additional space for water ballast and oil fuel. In the engine room, conventional Parsons' turbines were connected to twin shafts via single reduction gears. The turbines were supplied with steam at 14 bar by three single-ended oil-fired Scotch boilers working on the closed stokehold system. A novel safety feature allowed the engine room to be rapidly flooded to a depth of 150 mm with fire-fighting foam.

The accommodation provided for 800 first class and 600 second class passengers on both daylight and overnight sailings. There were staterooms each with twin berths and 19 twin berth cabins on the Promenade Deck. On the Main Deck were a further 16 single berth cabins and on the Lower Deck 20 more double berths. Each cabin had hot and cold water on tap, some had private lavatories, and all were heated by circulated warm air. Second class passengers had open segregated sleeping saloons, two for the men and two for the women. At the forward end of the Boat Deck was the first class smoke-room and bar which was adjacent to the main entrance hall. Separate ladies' and gents' lounges were situated forward on the Boat Deck and there was a 56 seater dining saloon on the Main Deck. All the first class accommodation was finished to a high standard with much use of mahogany and oak panelling, gilded carvings, and expensive upholstery, some of it black leather. However, second class passengers occupied a comparatively austere lounge on the Main Deck aft.

The maiden voyage took place on 13th March under the command of Captain E W Holt. Apart from the war years the ship remained on the Southampton to Channel Islands service for most of her career. She did one brief stint on the Newhaven to Dieppe route in the winter of 1946/47, and she also had occasional relief duties out of Weymouth. There were no significant incidents and few interruptions to service. The *Isle of Jersey* remained as built until withdrawn in 1960; she was converted on the Tyne to a pilgrim carrier and given the name *Libda*. She arrived at Libya only to be laid up and was later resold for demolition at La Spezia in 1963.

IRISH SEA STEAMERS AND THE DOVER TRAIN FERRIES

St Andrew (1932), alongside at Fishguard in the summer of 1963. (author)

With the exception of the Dover train ferries, all the remaining passenger turbine units built in the first half of the 1930s were for service in the Irish Sea. The Fishguard & Rosslare Railways & Harbours Company commissioned the sisters *St Andrew* and *St David* from Cammell Laird for the Fishguard service in 1932, as replacements for direct-drive steamers of the same name (see Chapter 2). The new ships had a gross tonnage of 2,702 and had the same turbine arrangement as the *St Patrick* (Chapter 7), but were equipped with four water tube boilers. Their service speed was 22 knots.

The *St Andrew* and *St David* were well proportioned vessels with excellent accommodation for just over 1,000 passengers. The first class single berth cabins were the largest and best furnished to be found on the crossing to Ireland. However, both vessels were prone to roll badly. During the war they were equipped as

Hospital Ships, attending first Dunkerque and then, in June 1943, the Allied Forces' battle front, whilst based at Malta. On 25th January 1944 the *St David* was lost off Anzio, her sister picking up many of the survivors. In September 1944 the *St Andrew* struck a mine returning from Ancona and was towed into Taranto. She was later repaired and refitted for commercial service on return to the UK in 1945.

The *St Andrew* led an uneventful life thereafter, partnering a new *St David* which was completed for the service in 1947 (see Chapter 9). The *St Andrew* was eventually withdrawn in 1967, at the age of 35, and sold for demolition.

Two new ships were also built for the Stranraer to Larne service of the London, Midland & Scottish Railway. Although not identical sisters, they had the same hull form. The first, the *Princess Margaret*, was launched from William Denny's yard on 21st January 1931 and was built at a cost of £179,000. She had twin sets of turbines and Babcock & Wilcox boilers which were coal fired. She was the largest ship then built for the route and had a gross tonnage of 2,523. First class accommodation was amidships with third class passengers on the Main Deck and the Lower Deck aft. For the first time, sleeping accommodation was offered to third class passengers (54 berths), and in all she could accommodate just over 1,200 passengers. On trials she managed nearly 21 knots at 269 revolutions per minute. Although originally fitted with a funnel cowl this was soon removed in common with all the other London, Midland & Scottish Railway steamers in the mid-1930s. On the arrival of the *Princess Margaret* into service a new express train was run from Glasgow which enabled passengers to avoid the long wait at Dumfries for the connecting train up from London.

A quasi-sister, the *Princess Maud* was delivered by Denny in 1934. She had the same machinery except that Erith-Roe mechanical stokers were employed in the stoke hold, the first cross-channel ship to be so equipped. Her main distinction,

Princess Maud (1933) was built for service at Stranraer but was transferred to Holyhead in the post-war years.
(Malcolm McRonald)

however, was that she was the first ever British ship to be equipped throughout with automatic sprinklers and a fire alarm system. She too had berths for both classes of passenger, and could accommodate a total of 1,480 passengers. Both ships were able to carry cattle and horses. Traffic grew on the route during the 1930s, and in 1938 the two ships carried a total of 219,000 passengers, 20,000 tons of cargo, 75,000 livestock and surprisingly 5,450 motor cars. It was this latter statistic which led to the building of the oil engined pioneer car ferry *Princess Victoria* in 1939.

Although the *Princess Victoria* was lost while on mine-laying duties in May 1940, the two passenger ships survived. The *Princess Margaret* had a short spell on the Heysham to Belfast route, and was present at the Normandy invasion, but otherwise remained on the Stranraer run throughout the war. The *Princess Maud*, however, was at Dunkerque, where a bomb penetrated her engine room killing several members of the crew, attended at St Valery, was involved in the D-Day Normandy landings and was the first steamer to enter Ostend with troops in 1944. In all, she carried nearly 1.4 million Allied troops during the war.

After the war, the *Princess Maud* stood in for her sister whilst she was overhauled and then transferred to Holyhead. The *Princess Margaret* remained at Stranraer; she was converted to burn oil fuel in 1952 and received major renovations to her public rooms in 1956. Her final sailing was 17th December 1961. She was sold for further service at Hong Kong; however, she was driven ashore during a Typhoon in August 1971 and eventually sold for demolition in 1975. Apparently, for some time after she first arrived in the Far East, she traded under her new name of *Macau* but retained Stranraer as her port of registry. It is also reported that her boilers were damaged on the delivery voyage to Hong Kong when brackish make-up water had to be used at Aden.

The *Princess Maud* was used at Holyhead as relief steamer, and deployed on additional sailings during peak periods. She also relieved on the Fishguard to Waterford and on the Stranraer to Larne routes. Like her sister, she was converted to burn oil fuel. The *Princess Maud* was not a popular ship on the Holyhead route, having no stabilisers and being relatively cramped. In due course, part of her first class accommodation, including a very fine smoke-room, was made over to second class in order to relieve congestion, and an observation lounge was built under the bridge. During peak summer weekends it was not uncommon for her to land and embark 2,000 passengers as well as clean ship during a 3 hour stay in port. Her last commercial voyage was on 5th September 1965, when she was sold for further service, eventually being broken up in 1973.

The Heysham to Belfast route also received a new ship. This was the *Duke of York*, which represented the last of the spate of new building by the railways since their regrouping in 1923. The three new Dukes placed on the route in 1928 (Chapter 4) had been so successful that traffic had increased considerably on the route, and the elderly *Duke of Abercorn*, formerly the *Curraghmore*, had been drafted in as a temporary measure until the new ship could be built.

The *Duke of York* was built at Belfast by Harland & Wolff, and had more emphasis on cargo carrying than the 1928 Dukes, but offered the same speed and passenger facilities. As such, she could maintain 21 knots and made the 200 km overnight crossing in about 7 hours. For the first time the difference between first and third class was small, and the standard of accommodation for both was very high. She could accommodate 1,500 passengers and had berths for 139 first class passengers in single and double cabins, and 228 third class passengers in 1, 2, 3 or 4 berth cabins. The first class saloon and lounge were both on the Bridge Deck, smoking rooms for both classes were on the Promenade Deck and the third class lounge was aft on the Main Deck.

At the outbreak of war, the *Duke of York* became a troop transport, attended at Dunkerque and was later converted into a Landing Ship Infantry for 250 troops with ten assault craft. Temporarily renamed *Duke of Wellington*, she took

Duke of York (1935), seen as built for the Heysham to Belfast service. (Mike Walker collection)

part in the raid on Dieppe and the Normandy landings before taking up trooping duties at Harwich. Following a major refit, she returned to Heysham in late 1947. However, in May 1948 she transferred to Harwich following the loss of the *Prague* while refitting on the Clyde (Chapter 4). In July 1950 the *Duke of York* did a brief stint on the Southampton to Cherbourg route before returning to her builders for extensive refurbishment to fit her for the Harwich service. She was converted to burn oil fuel and exchanged her two funnels for a single large elliptical funnel. Her passenger accommodation was rearranged and extended into what had been the Number 2 hold. There were now berths for 359 first class and 160 second class passengers. The forward cranes were removed and the forecastle extended over the former crane platform. Her gross tonnage was now 4,190.

She returned to Harwich in May 1951, but had a short spell at Holyhead during the summer. On 6th May 1953, in the early hours of the morning and some 65 km off Harwich, she collided with an American government owned freighter which sliced away the fore part of the *Duke of York*. Three people died in the incident, and the ship was towed stern first into Harwich. In 1954 a new bow section was fitted by Palmer's on the Tyne, giving her a more modern raked prow. Now with a gross tonnage of 4,325 she continued to run on the Harwich to Hook of Holland service for a further 9 years; she carried out her last inbound sailing on 20th July 1963, arriving at Harwich dressed overall. Sold to Chandris Lines of Greece, she was then used as a cruise liner in the Mediterranean until withdrawn in 1972.

The London, Midland & Scottish Railway had placed an order with the Fairfield Shipbuilding & Engineering Company in 1939 for two 5,000 ton turbine driven steamers as replacements for the *Scotia, Hibernia* and *Cambria* (Chapter 3) on the Holyhead to Dun Laoghaire route. However, work on the order was never started and the

The post-war motor ship *Hibernia* (1948) was originally ordered in 1939, one of pair of turbine steamers. (author)

intervention of the war nullified the contract. In the event, two motor ships, the *Hibernia* and *Cambria,* were eventually built for the service by Harland & Wolff in the late 1940s.

On the South Coast, in the early 1930s, the Southern Railway had the vision of sending through-trains, rather than just foot passengers and goods, to Continental destinations. It was a vision which was finally completed in the early 1990s when the permanent way of the Channel Tunnel was completed. In the 1930s, however, the idea was to carry wagons lits on night trains between London and Paris, using the train ferry technology which had earlier been pioneered at Richborough near Sandwich and later at Harwich for freight.

There were considerable engineering problems to overcome, not least the means of loading long passenger carriages onto the ship over the stern in a harbour with an 8 m tide. To this end, a drawbridge complete with track was assembled at the end of a newly commissioned Train Ferry Dock. Here the water could be pumped up to a constant level despite the tide, but only when the considerable permeability of the surrounding Chalk had been sealed, a job which took until 1936 to accomplish successfully. In the meantime, three specially built steamers had been designed, ordered and constructed and then laid up to await completion of the dock. Out of fifteen tenders, the contract for the three new ships was awarded to Swan Hunter & Wigham Richardson during April 1933. The first two keels were laid down in October and the third followed in November. The ships were launched as follows: *Twickenham Ferry*, 15th March 1934; *Hampton Ferry*, 30th July 1934; and *Shepperton Ferry*, 23rd October 1934.

The three ships were delivered between July 1934 and March 1935, and during trials were found to be top heavy with an undue tendency to roll. Additional ballast in the form of 200 tons of old railway lines was cemented into the lower car carrying deck of each ship (room for 25 cars). In addition, as the three new ships had replaced French flag vessels, it was agreed that the *Twickenham Ferry* would lose her London registry and hoist the French flag. It was 'Le Twic' which had the honour of operating the inaugural inbound service on 6th October 1936, whilst the *Hampton Ferry* ran the outward service. The *Shepperton Ferry* completed her maiden commercial voyage in November after a defect to her bow rudder had been rectified; her sisters were later also modified for this same defect.

It was originally intended that the train ferries would run between Dover and Boulogne. However, on advice from French railway officials, the service was redesigned, with Dunkerque as the Continental terminal. There was accommodation for 700 passengers and either 12 Wagons Lits carriages or 40 standard goods trucks. The Night Ferry service left either port in the early hours and enabled a through service between London and Paris, and after the war also to Brussels. There were troughs between the lines to receive sewage from the Wagons Lits, and the troughs were regularly sluiced with sea water. The anthracite stoves in the carriages were banked down with damp fuel prior to the ferry crossing.

The three ships were equipped with twin pairs of Parsons' turbines and steam was generated in four Yarrow water tube boilers with automatic coal feed. Coal was the preferred fuel due to the proximity of the Kent Coalfield; however, all were adapted to burn oil fuel in 1947. They each had a pair of tall funnels, one on either side of the Promenade Deck. They had a service speed of only 16 knots and many of their masters claimed that the ships were underpowered, especially with regard to their considerable top hamper. They were never very steady ships in a running sea, and many services were cancelled for fear of trucks and wagons being derailed as the ships pitched and rolled across the Channel.

The train ferry service was suspended on 25th August 1939 when all three vessels were requisitioned for minelaying. They were released from these duties in time to take up station between Stranraer and Larne the following year in support of the many military manoeuvres that were then scheduled in Northern Ireland. Towards the end of the war they received large gantries over the stern

Twickenham Ferry (1934) reversing up to the Train Ferry Dock at Dover. (Malcolm McRonald)

Hampton Ferry (1934), seen at Dover in August 1965. It was this ship that served at Stranraer for much of the 1950s.

Shepperton Ferry (1934) leaving Dover in July 1968. (both photos, author)

for delivering rolling stock to Continental ports.

The three ships later reverted to civilian duties and the full service to Dunkerque was reinstated during 1947. Both the British flag vessels spent time at Stranraer in post war years, acting as stern loading road vehicle and passenger ferries, the *Hampton Ferry* throughout much of the 1950s and the *Shepperton Ferry* for relief services through until the early 1960s. During the 1960s, they tended to carry more road vehicles than rail, and were also adapted for service to the rail linkspan at Zeebrugge, which had previously only been served from Harwich. The three elderly steamers were successively withdrawn and sold for demolition between 1969 and 1974. The *Shepperton Ferry* carried out her last trip to Dunkerque in the evening of 25th August 1972, the *Twickenham Ferry* on 5th May 1974, when her boilers finally expired, whereas the *Hampton Ferry* had already been displaced by new tonnage back in 1969. The *Hampton Ferry* was sold in 1970 for demolition at Faslane, but there she was reboilered and sold on to the Chandris Line as the *Tre Arddur*, only being demolished in 1973 after a long lay up in Piraeus.

The Duke of York

As built, the *Duke of York* had a gross tonnage of 3,743, net of 1,547 and a deadweight of 750 tons. Her draft was 4 m and her length was 106 m. There were eight main watertight bulkheads, with two holds forward and one aft, boiler and engine rooms, a space forward of the boiler room for fresh water and ballast tanks and a space aft for ballast and fire sprinkler water. There were three decks: the Lower Deck was divided by the machinery spaces, the Main Deck, and the Bridge Deck which consisted of a forecastle bridge and poop.

The machinery consisted of the standard arrangement of Parsons' single reduction geared turbines. Each set had an impulse-reaction high pressure turbine and a reaction low pressure turbine, which together generated a power of 6,000 kilowatts, with astern blades in the same casings. Steam was generated in four Babcock & Wilcox water tube boilers to a pressure of 16 bar under closed stokehold forced draft. The boilers were coal fired, with Erith-Roe mechanical stokers fed under gravity from a bunker which was situated between the two funnels.

The forward well deck had rolling hatch covers which were in two sections and could slide away to starboard. Above the Bridge Deck level was the upper forecastle and upper bridge, the Promenade Deck, and a short Boat Deck aft, although there was a long Boat Deck over the Promenade Deck amidships. The main Promenade Deck was partially enclosed in glass panels. There were large cargo doors to port and smaller ones to starboard as she was designed to load port side to the quay. There was a 10 ton derrick on the main mast and two electric cranes. There were stalls for 316 head of cattle in the forward 'tween decks, and general cargo could be stowed in the forward holds and after 'tween decks whilst additional cargo space for baggage and motor vehicles was available in the wells. The *Duke of York* had a double bottom for her full length and was equipped with a bow rudder. The steering gear and windlasses were electrically driven. There was an astern navigating bridge abaft the funnels. There were eight life boats swung under luffing davits.

The ship underwent considerable alteration during her military and peace time duties (see pages 70/71). On sale to the Chandris Line in 1963 she was put in hand by Smiths Dock at Middlesbrough where the Promenade Deck was lengthened and modifications to cabins and steelwork made ready for the installation of swimming pools. The conversion was completed in Greece and as the *Fantasia* she was given cabin accommodation for 381 passengers with 1, 2, 3 and 4 berth cabins on the Diana and Venus (formerly Lower) Deck; 1, 2 and 3 berth cabins on the Minerva (Main) Deck and single and double cabins on the Lido (Promenade) Deck. There were two swimming pools on the Lido Deck, and closed circuit television and air conditioning throughout. All the public rooms were at the after end of the decks, and there were four bars, one called the Eldorado which also had a dance floor. The main restaurant on the Minerva Deck extended the full width of the ship. The original machinery saw her through to the end. The cruise ship *Fantasia* had a career of nine years and was then laid up for a further two; the former *Duke of York* was sold for demolition at the age of 39 years.

WORLD WAR II AND POST-WAR RECONSTRUCTION

In the late 1930s the railways were again planning new tonnage. Although the Belgian state ferries and Coast Lines Seaways were by then firmly committed to motor driven ships, the railways stayed with the single reduction geared turbine (with the exception of the London, Midland & Scottish Railway's motor driven car ferry *Princess Victoria*). These were still the days when the operator approached a shipbuilder with a specification for speed and capacity, and a preference for machinery type, and the shipbuilder, rather than the operator, produced the design for the ship. Nevertheless, each operator developed its own distinctive design style through the iterative process of design approval that ensued before the keel could be laid.

The Southern Railway wanted a fast, large capacity ferry to take over the Golden Arrow service from the *Canterbury*, which was then considered to be 'out of date'. To this end, an order was placed with Denny for a three decked steamer capable of 22 knots. This was the *Invicta*, a large ship with a gross tonnage of 4,178 and accommodation for 900 first class and 400 second class passengers. She was driven by two twin sets of Parsons turbines fed by two coal fired Yarrow boilers with mechanical stokers. She was launched without ceremony on

Invicta (1940), leaving Dover on the Golden Arrow service to Calais, in the summer of 1965. (author)

14th December 1939 and delivered on 1st July 1940, then to be laid up at anchor in the Clyde. She had cost £290,000 to build. Meanwhile, plans by the Southern Railway for Dennys to build a replacement for the Southampton steamer *Lorina* had to be shelved.

Taken over by the Admiralty in 1941, the *Invicta* was fitted with anti-mine degaussing equipment and converted to a Landing Ship Infantry. She was painted black with buff upperworks and equipped with anti-aircraft guns and one larger gun behind the bridge. She was involved in the Dieppe raid in August 1941 and later in the Normandy landings. In December 1945 she was decommissioned and immediately placed on the Dover to Calais route on the forces leave service. The ship was returned to the Southern Railway in 1946 when she was completely refitted and converted to burn oil fuel. Following a publicity cruise, the *Invicta* finally entered the Golden Arrow service on 15th October 1946.

The *Invicta* was the largest cross-Channel ship in service until 1966 when the Belgian ferry *Prinses Paola* was commissioned. Throughout her peacetime career of 26 years, the *Invicta* stayed on the Dover-Calais route for which she was designed. Most days the ship was only in steam for five hours, leaving Dover at 12.30 hours and returning by 17.30 hours. In peak periods she was also scheduled for an evening trip to Boulogne returning to Dover by 09.00 hours. The *Invicta* had a very distinctive character and a unique style, the latter perhaps best characterised by the comfortable green leather settees in her first class lounge. Her final crossing was on 8th August 1972, after which she was laid up at Newhaven, pending sale for demolition.

The *Invicta* was just one of the 59 single reduction geared British registered turbine steamers to go to war. Of these a total of 15 were lost in action (Table 4). There were also 15 British direct-drive turbine steamers left in service in 1939 and all of these, save one, survived the war.

At the end of the war, plans for the replacement for the *Lorina*, which as it happened had been lost in the war, were resuscitated and an order placed with Dennys for another three deck steamer. This was the *Falaise*, which was launched on 25th October 1946, ostensibly for the Channel Islands service but ultimately pressed into service on the St Malo route. Post-war material shortages delayed her trials until the following summer, and her maiden voyage from Southampton to St Malo eventually took place on 14th June 1947. Until 1951, she had to anchor off St Malo in the River Rance and her passengers were ferried ashore in vedettes. The *Falaise* was powered by the usual double set of twin Parsons turbines with steam generated by two oil-fired Foster Wheeler boilers and delivered at 31 bar. Her design speed was just over 20 knots. She was equipped with a bow rudder and Denny-Brown stabilisers. The total cost of the ship was £560,000.

The *Falaise* was essentially a smaller version of the *Invicta*. Accommodation on the *Falaise* was designed for 940 first class and 510 second class passengers, and there were sleeping berths for 338. With a gross tonnage of 3,710 she was the largest railway ship then operating out of Southampton. The *Falaise* quickly settled down to a routine of night sailing out and day sailing back, and with her spacious and comfortable accommodation and modern fittings she soon became popular with the travelling public. The first class smokeroom was under the bridge and there were two first class lounges on the Promenade Deck. On the Main Deck was a dining saloon which could seat 112. During the late 1940s and throughout the 1950s she was used for a series of weekend cruises to Holland, Belgium, France and the Channel Islands. In 1960 she received considerable attention to her public rooms and her wheelhouse was extended forward. She otherwise remained on the St Malo route until the route was closed in 1964, with occasional relief services elsewhere.

The *Falaise* was then converted at Vickers Hebburn yard into a stern loading car ferry at a cost of some £350,000. Only the first class smokeroom and the after lounges remained intact. The Main Deck was gutted and the Upper Deck forward cabins turned into crew accommodation and a tea bar installed. The section aft of the funnel casing became part of the garage and the after part of the Main Deck was cut away to give extra height to the new Car Deck. The third class lounges on the

Falaise (1946) in her new role as a car ferry, seen leaving Newhaven, wearing the joint Anglo-French funnel colours. (author)

Promenade Deck became a self service cafeteria. The shelters were cut away from the bridge wings, and finally she received a new colour scheme whereby the black hull was raised by one deck level.

In this guise, the *Falaise* now had accommodation for 700 one-class passengers and 100 cars, and she was one of the first ferries to be equipped with airline type seating. After conversion, it was found that the ship would sheer to one side unexpectedly whilst manoeuvring in harbour, and attempts to rectify this included fitting side plates either side of the rudder and extending the rudder but neither was effective. Eventually, in January 1968, success was achieved when a steel plate was fitted to fill in the adjacent deadwood area of the keel.

The car ferry *Falaise* was initially used on the Newhaven to Dieppe route, commencing on 1st June 1964, and later served on the Weymouth to Channel Islands service, commencing on 30th May 1973, but with occasional stand-in work at Dover. Towards the end of 1974 she suffered serious mechanical failure which was considered unworthy of repair; she was quickly sold for demolition.

The Isle of Man Steam Packet Company had lost its three newest ships plus the older *King Orry* during the war; others were unfit for return to civilian duties. The company immediately set about a programme of rebuilding to a design that was based on the pre-war twins *Fenella* and *Tynwald*, both of which were war casualties. Five almost identical ships were built by Cammell Laird between 1946 and 1951. Affectionately referred to as the buses (i.e. they don't just come in ones!), the ships had the same basic hull form and dimensions, and also the same machinery. They were 99 m long with a beam of 14 m and the gross tonnage ranged from

King Orry (1946), seen approaching the Mersey in August 1962. (Malcolm McRonald)

Tynwald (1947) arriving at Douglas in July 1966. (author)

Mona's Queen (1946) was the first of the post-war Isle of Man boats to be sold. (Malcolm McRonald)

2,485 to 2,495. They had raked stems, cruiser sterns, two pole masts and a single funnel topped by a cowl. They had the conventional pair of twin Parsons turbines receiving steam at 17 bar from two Babcock & Wilcox water tube boilers which were oil-fired on the closed stokehold system of forced draught with air supplied by two electric fans. The engines generated a power of 6,300 kilowatts, and drove twin shafts via single reduction gears to give them an operating speed of 21 knots. Astern power amounted to 70% of the ahead power, and each ship had a bow rudder. The first pair was the *King Orry* and *Mona's Queen* which cost £402,000 and £405,000 to build in 1946; followed by the *Tynwald* in 1947 at a cost of £462,000, the *Snaefell* at £504,000 in 1948 and the *Mona's Isle* which cost £570,000 in 1951.

The passenger accommodation on the quins was comfortable, designed for two classes, and of a high standard, particularly with the winter services in mind. In fact the *Mona's Queen* created quite a contrast to the austere surroundings of post-war Merseyside when she first lay alongside Princes Landing Stage. The ships could accommodate 2,200 passengers in two classes, and had the normal public rooms as well as eight private cabins which could be pre-booked.

Aboard each ship there was a large first class lounge forward on the Promenade Deck extending the full width of the ship. The first class dining room spanned the width of the Main Deck with seating for 84, and there were two sleeping lounges on the Lower Deck with sofa-berths for 80 passengers. There was also a smoking room and a ladies lounge with a further 42 sofa-berths. Minor modifications and improvements were made with each succeeding ship, always for the increased comfort of the passengers. Third class passengers had sleeping saloons at the aft end of the Lower Deck, a 60 seater dining saloon at the forward end of the Lower Deck and a ladies room on the Shelter Deck. There was also a third class lounge and a smokeroom on the Main Deck, and a selection of buffets and bars. In addition 200 sofa-berths were also available to third class passengers.

The order for the *King Orry* and *Mona's Queen* was placed before the end of the war on 1st February 1945 and they were launched respectively on 22nd November 1945 and 5th February 1946. The hulls were transversely framed and riveted throughout

Mona's Isle (1951), heading down the Mersey in May 1967 on passage to Douglas. (author)

with seven watertight bulkheads. The maiden voyage of the *King Orry* was on 18th April 1946 from Liverpool to Douglas under the command of Captain Albert Whiteway. The ship was quickly recognised as a great advance on the pre-war *Tynwald* and *Fenella*, particularly from a passenger point of view with the continuous Upper Deck and glass screened Main Deck or Shelter Deck. The *King Orry* was fitted with a flying bridge above the wheelhouse which was used when going astern. This was extended to the full width of the ship in the winter of 1947/48. Later, in 1954, she received radar, and in May 1960 the Bridge Deck was extended by 7 m so that additional life rafts could be carried. Her appearance was greatly improved in May 1961 when her funnel cowl was removed – none of her sisters were allowed this treatment.

The *Mona's Queen* managed well over 21 knots on trials and took up service with a maiden voyage to Douglas on 26th June 1946 under Captain Bridson. She was to suffer boiler trouble which eventually led to her returning to her builders, Cammell Laird, in February 1953, followed by a major machinery refit a year later. It was this ship which undertook the final outward Fleetwood service in September 1962 flying the signal 'With regret, goodbye, Fleetwood'.

The *Tynwald* was launched on 24th March 1947 and carried out her maiden voyage on 31st July. She had a slightly different appearance as the Upper Deck was rounded off to make more deck space, and a greater part of the Main Deck was screened by glass. Whereas the first two ships of the class only had a well for loading cars on the starboard side, the *Tynwald* and later vessels had one on both sides to avoid starboard to quay only loading. In her early years she often deputised for the *King Orry* and *Mona's Queen* on the winter service. The *Snaefell* followed down the ways on 3rd March 1948 and was in service under Captain A Whiteway on 24th July. Her glass screening was even more extensive than that of the *Tynwald*. Between 19th and 24th September that year, she ran evening cruises from Fleetwood to view the Blackpool illuminations then newly restored after the war. She later reopened the Dublin service in 1950.

The *Snaefell* (1948) leaving Princes Landing Stage, Liverpool. (author)

The last of the 'buses', the *Mona's Isle*, was launched on 12th October 1950 and achieved nearly 22 knots on trials on the Clyde. Her maiden voyage was on 22nd March 1951, again with Captain Whiteway in charge. Each of the ships was involved in minor skirmishes, including collision with fishing boats at Fleetwood, impact with Princes Stage at Liverpool and stranding at Peel, from which the *Mona's Isle* had to be towed back to Liverpool for repairs lasting several months.

The first of the ships to be disposed of was the *Mona's Queen* which was sold for further service in the Mediterranean in October 1962. She was disposed of before the pre-war *Ben-my-Chree* and *Lady of Mann* because she would release more money, although her hull was said to be in poor condition, and because the older ships had a larger passenger capacity for peak period use. As the *Carina*, and later the *Fiesta*, she had 40 double berth cabins, and 40 four-berth cabins each with its own en-suite, plus reclining seating for a further 325. There was a swimming pool, complete air conditioning, a 300 seater restaurant, and as the *Carina* there was drive-on facilities for 60 cars. The *King Orry* carried out her last service inbound from Llandudno to Liverpool on 31st August 1975 and proceeded to Glasson Dock near Lancaster in November to await demolition. She had steamed 516,770 miles and carried 3,325,000 passengers, 23,393 cars and 43,372 motor bikes (carried on the Main Deck), in a total of 7,412 crossings including 259 positioning voyages. In January 1976 she became quite a celebrity when she broke her moorings at Glasson Dock and stranded on a mud bank on a very high tide in a Force 10 gale. She could not be moved until the next spring tides, and was eventually towed to Rochester for breaking up.

The *Tynwald* finished with the 18.00 hours departure from Douglas to Liverpool on 26th August 1974 and left the Mersey for demolition in

Stern first approach to Folkestone. The *St Patrick* (1947) is seen in July 1968, in bound from Boulogne. (author)

February 1975. The *Snaefell* was laid up throughout 1977 and was sold for demolition the following year. The *Mona's Isle* was responsible for a number of interesting charters such as Barrow to Llandudno and the Workington Town Band charter which required skillful matching of times with the tide. Her final charter was a round the island cruise to celebrate the 150th Anniversary of the launch of the first *Mona's Isle* in August 1980. She was then withdrawn and sold for demolition, finally leaving the Mersey on 30th October that year.

The Fishguard & Rosslare Railways & Harbours Company also needed replacements for war losses and orders were placed with Cammell Laird for two ships. The ships were designed as enlarged and updated versions of the 1930s pair they replaced, and not dissimilar to the *St Julien* and *St Helier* dating from 1925, although the new ships only had one funnel; they also inherited the same names and services, the *St David* for the overnight Fishguard to Rosslare route and the *St Patrick* for the daytime Weymouth to Channel Islands services. They were launched on 6th February and 20th May 1947 respectively, and together they represented an investment of well over £1 million. Maiden voyages of both ships took place under the command of Captain R R Pitman.

The machinery for the two ships was the conventional twin sets of Parsons' turbines with three Babcock and Wilcox boilers. Their service speed was 20 knots, which they achieved at 260 revolutions per minute, and an economic overnight speed of 15 knots was achieved at 175 revolutions per minute. Both ships were built with bow rudders, but neither had stabilisers. As the *St David* was a dedicated overnight ship, the internal layout of the two ships was slightly different. Both ships could accommodate 1,300 passengers; the *St David* in two classes with 353 berths and space for 50 cars, whereas the *St Patrick* could only carry 28 cars, with

St David (1947) arriving at Heysham from Dun Laoghaire in 1970. Note the Great Western Railway coat of arms on the bow. (author)

the extra space committed to third-class passenger accommodation. Outwardly, the only difference was the number and size of the windows on the Promenade Deck.

Unlike the Southern Railway's *Invicta* and *Falaise*, the new *St David* and *St Patrick* were traditional two-deck ships with a part Lower Deck fore and aft of the engine and the boiler room spaces. The accommodation was grouped together amidships with cargo holds forward and aft. Both ships set new standards on the respective routes, the *St David* running as partner to the pre-war *St Andrew*. As there was no rationing in the Republic of Ireland, food was plentiful aboard the *St David* and passengers would head for the dining saloon for Limerick ham, eggs, Irish bread and real butter, before retiring to their berths! The *St Patrick* was finished internally in rust, cream and green and there was a large inlaid map in the vestibule showing the Great Western Railway crest and area of operation.

The *St Patrick* spent her first 16 summers on the Channel Islands services and her winters either laid up at Fishguard or acting as relief. In 1961 she was converted to one-class only, a cafeteria was installed, and most of the cabin accommodation removed. The third class sleeping accommodation became crew quarters, and part of the forward hold was converted into a lounge. In addition, the stairways were fire-proofed and the wooden inlay in the vestibule removed, the transformation costing in all some £91,000. With new ships then on the route, she became third ship but still played a part in the mail service, with St Malo trips and excursion work as well.

On 4th December 1963 the *St Patrick* transferred to Southampton and took up the Le Havre service until it was closed on 10th May 1964, whereupon she took up the St Malo route until that too was terminated on 27th September 1964. She then received minor alterations, including the provision of large gangway doors in each side, and transferred to Dover-Calais in December 1964, and to Folkestone-Boulogne the following year. She remained on this route until withdrawn in 1971, her final return trip being on 26th September. During this latter period she carried out a number of excursions including trips to the Channel Islands. Sold for further service under the Greek flag, she was eventually scrapped in 1980.

The *St David* remained at Fishguard until 1969. During her first year of service she had spent one month on the Weymouth route, but was otherwise a one-service ship. In 1964 holes were cut in her sides below the after well deck, to allow access for 66 cars on one deck. The work also included extensive fire resistance and protection work. Thereafter, she operated three crossings per week in winter and two per day in summer. In 1969 she finally left Fishguard and worked out of Holyhead, going up to Heysham when fire damaged the Anglesey railway bridge in 1970. She was sold in 1971 but, after prolonged lay up in Piraeus, was later broken up.

New tonnage for Townsend Car Ferries was acquired in 1946 in the shape of the former River-class frigate *Halladale*, built in 1944 by A & J Inglis. Most of the River-, Loch- and Bay-class frigates had been equipped with diesel engines, but the *Halladale* was one of only six to be given conventional twin high and low pressure turbines connected via single reduction gears to twin shafts. Although she was of light construction with a high length to breadth ratio of 8.3, she was seen as an ideal successor to the ageing steam reciprocating engined *Forde*, a former minesweeper, completed in 1919, which had pioneered the company's Dover to Calais car and passenger service in direct competition with the Southern Railway.

The *Halladale* was bought from the Admiralty for £15,000 and was converted for commercial service by the Cork Dockyard Company for a further £77,000. Her first commercial voyage was on 6th April 1950, although the service was suspended four days later until 19th May, after the ship had grounded in Calais harbour. Although capable of 20 knots, her operational speed was usually just over 17 knots. The ship had a gross tonnage of only 1,370 but could accommodate 55 cars and 368 passengers. She was able to commence roll-on loading at Calais in June 1951, and at Dover in June 1953 as link spans became available. Although the *Halladale* always looked like a converted frigate, she gave sterling service to her owners and was eventually retired in November 1961 after which she was sold for further service out of Sweden and later Venezuela.

The last steamer to be delivered to the London & North Eastern Railway before the nationalisation of the railways in 1948 was the *Arnhem*. She was a product of John Brown and like the newer Great Western Railway ships was a two decked ship with a part third deck fore and aft of the engine spaces. She also had four holds, two forward and two aft. The *Arnhem* was launched into the Clyde on 7th November 1946, and entered the night service between Harwich and the Hook of Holland on 26th May 1947. The name derived from the town in Holland at which the Germans fought with the British 1st Airborne Division in September 1944. The ship had conventional twin pairs of turbines on two shafts with two Yarrow type water tube boilers which were oil fuelled. Her design speed was 21 knots.

Accommodation aboard the *Arnhem* was second to none even though she was fitted out as a single-class ship. Her total passenger complement was only 750, and there were four suites available plus 319 cabins. Her accommodation was rearranged in 1954 to include second class passengers, whereupon she had a reduced passenger capacity of 675, but increased berths for 576; her gross tonnage rose from 4,891 to 5,008 during this adjustment. Her running mate was the elderly *Prague* (see Chapter 4), but when she was gutted by fire during refit a replacement was urgently sought by the newly formed British Transport Commission. This was the *Duke of York* (Chapter 8), which was originally built for the Heysham to Belfast service. In addition, an order was placed for a new vessel as consort to the *Arnhem*.

The new ship was named the *Amsterdam*, and was to all intents and purposes a repeat of the

Arnhem (1947) on the night berth at Parkeston Quay, in the summer of 1965. (author)

Amsterdam (1950) seen approaching Harwich on the day-tme service from Hook of Holland. (author)

Maid of Orleans (1949) arriving at Dover in September 1973. The aft hatch cover is raised ready for unloading. (author)

Arnhem. There were a number of minor differences, not least outwardly, as the new ship had her lifeboats swung on gravity davits and had fewer windows on the Upper Deck. Inwardly, the main difference was that the accommodation was designed around two classes from the outset, and she was licensed to carry a total of 675 passengers, with 321 first class and 236 second class berths. She was launched at Clydebank on 19th January 1950 and entered service on 11th June that year under the command of Captain C. Baxter.

The two ships sustained the overnight mail service with support from the *Duke of York* until 1968, when they were overtaken by diesel driven car ferries. The *Arnhem* carried out her final inbound service on 26th April 1968 and was promptly sold for demolition. The *Amsterdam* completed her final round trip on 8th November 1968 and was sold the following April for £200,000 for further service in the Mediterranean cruise market. Here she had a career of nine years as the Chandris Line cruise ship *Fiorita*, and was then sold on for use as a hotel ship in Turkey during which service she eventually sank at her moorings.

The first steamer to be ordered by the newly formed British Transport Commission in 1948 was the *Maid of Orleans*, designed specifically for the Folkestone to Boulogne route. She was also intended for use on the Dover to Calais and daytime Southampton to St Malo services, the latter much as the *Isle of Thanet* had done in pre-war summer weekends. She was one of the last cross-channel ships designed with conventional twin-paired Parsons turbine drive to twin shafts, although concession was made to new engineering developments by casing the turbine units in asbestos cement.

The *Maid of Orleans* had two oil-fired Foster Wheeler boilers which provided steam at 19 bar at a temperature of 260°C. She was launched from the yard of William Denny on 17th September 1948 and, on trials, attained a speed of over 22 knots at 274 revolutions per minute. She was built with Denny-Brown stabilisers. The new ship was 104 m long by 15 m broad (a length to breadth ratio of 6.8) and had a gross tonnage of 3,444.

The maiden voyage of the *Maid of Orleans* took place out of Folkestone on 23rd June 1949. She had accommodation for 1,404 passengers in two classes. She was a three decked ship: A Deck, which was the Promenade Deck, offered a spacious smoke room bar, B Deck had the lounge and restaurant and C Deck had day cabins as well as the second class cafeteria. In addition, there were holds fore and aft which amongst other cargo allowed up to 35 cars to be craned aboard.

From the 1949 season onwards, the *Maid of Orleans* was joined in the summer by the *Canterbury* (Chapter 4) to maintain the Folkestone to Boulogne service. This lasted until 1965 when the *St Patrick* was substituted after the *Canterbury* had been withdrawn from service. Throughout this period the *Maid of Orleans* stood in for the *Invicta* as winter relief for the Golden Arrow service, and relieved other services in the Dover Strait as required.

The only significant alterations made to the *Maid of Orleans* took place in the winter of 1958/59, when her funnel was lengthened by the addition of a domed cowl to prevent downdraught of fumes.

Perhaps the highlight of her career came in 1972 when the *Invicta* was withdrawn and the *Maid of Orleans* herself inherited the Golden Arrow service out of Dover on 9th August; glory was to be short lived as she closed the service on 30th September. She remained on the Dover to Calais route thereafter, although without the prestigious title, and also carried out reliefs on the Weymouth to Channel Islands routes. Her final sailing to Calais was on 27th September 1975 under the command of Captain George Sutcliffe; she carried out an excursion to Boulogne the next day then retired to lay up at Newhaven, pending disposal. The *Maid of Orleans* had led an impeccable career without major incident or accident, and remains a fitting epitaph for the single reduction geared twin-paired-turbine cross-channel steamer.

Table 4 : British registered cross-channel turbine steamers lost in World War II

ship	built	cause of loss	date	position
Archangel; ex-St Petersburg*	1910	bomb	16th May 1941	57°55′N 02°03′W
Normannia	1911	bomb	30th May 1940	off Dunkerque
King Orry	1913	bomb	30th May 1940	off Dunkerque
Paris	1913	bomb	2nd June 1940	51°11′N 02°07′E
Maid of Orleans	1918	torpedo	28th June 1944	50°10′N 00°40′W
Lorina	1918	bomb	29th May 1940	Dunkerque Roads
Scotia	1920	bomb	1st June 1940	51°07′N 02°10′E
St Briac	1924	mine	12th March 1942	off Aberdeen
Maid of Kent	1925	bomb	21st May 1940	Dieppe Harbour
Amsterdam	1930	mine	7th August 1944	49°25′N 00°35′W
St Patrick	1930	bomb	13th June 1941	52°04′N 05°25′W
Brighton	1931	bomb	24th May 1940	Dieppe Harbour
St David	1932	bomb	24th January 1944	41°10′N 12°21′E
Mona's Queen	1934	mine	29th May 1940	off Dunkerque
Tynwald	1937	mine	12th November 1942	off Bougie, Algeria
Fenella	1937	bomb	29th May 1940	Dunkerque

* Direct-drive turbine

The former British flag ferry *Corregidor*, ex-*Engadine* (1911), was also lost, as was the *Rosaura*, ex-*Dieppe* (1905), but which had since been converted to diesel. The *St Denis*, ex-*Munich* (1908), was scuttled at Amsterdam but later raised and used as a minelayer by the Germans.

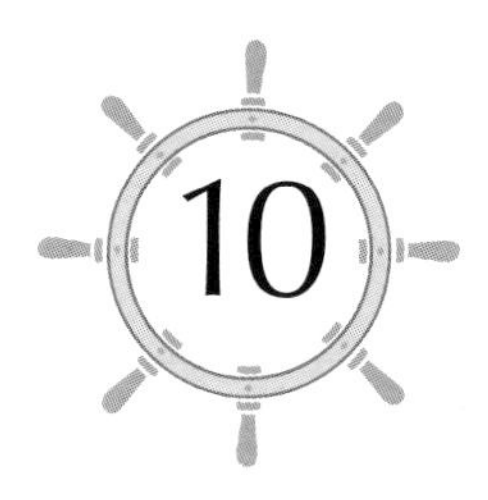

PAMETRADA AND DOUBLE REDUCTION GEARS

Many technical innovations were forthcoming from the effort of war, but it usually took a considerable time for them to filter down to everyday life. This was largely because of the immediate need to produce only to pre-war standards in order to overcome war losses. In the case of the marine turbine, it was realised when the Royal Navy was working alongside the Americans in the Pacific, that the fuel consumption of the British turbine ships was considerably greater than that of the Americans. A committee was set up after the war to investigate and as a result, a research association, the Parsons and Marine Engineering Turbine Research and Development Association (Pametrada), was formed as a component of the Department of Scientific and Industrial Research. It was partly funded by Government and partly by industry. The aim was to develop simple but rugged turbines with the ability to withstand considerable degrees of stress without undue complications.

Pametrada quickly produced designs for more efficient, compact and lighter units than the pre-war turbines. Attention was also focused on cross-channel requirements where full power is required shortly after leaving the quayside. Nevertheless, pre-war turbine designs, many little modified since the early 1920s, were still being fitted to post-war ships and it was only in the early 1950s that the shipbuilders had the opportunity to offer the new designs. The Pametrada turbines were designed to operate at higher revolutions, and the more complex double reduction gearing, developed originally for cargo steamers, was introduced to cross-channel ships as the couple between engines and shafts. The reduction ratio was typically 1: 20.

The first cross-channel ship to benefit from this post-war research and development was the fast turbine steamer *Brighton*, built for the Newhaven to Dieppe route. She was another product of William Denny and by the standards of the day was relatively small, being some 2,875 tons gross. However, she remains the most powerful turbine steamer ever built for UK cross channel duties. Her passenger complement was 850 first class and 600 third class, and she required a crew of 79 including 35 stewards. She was launched on 7th October 1949 and undertook her trials during late April 1950. The *Brighton* is recorded as achieving over 23 knots at 355 revolutions per minute, but was more than capable of maintaining her design speed of 24 knots. As such, she was the last of the fast turbine steamers ever to be commissioned.

Her machinery was somewhat hybrid. Two oil-fired Foster Wheeler boilers supplied steam at 340°C at a pressure of 31 bar to a pair of Pametrada design turbines each driving an independent shaft via single reduction gears. With the astern entry to Newhaven in mind, she was given reverse turbines capable of 85% of the forward power. The *Brighton* took up station at Newhaven alongside the *Worthing*, another product of Denny dating from 1928 (Chapter 4) but also capable of the high speeds required of this long crossing.

The *Brighton* continued on the Newhaven to Dieppe route without major incident until 1965. During the winters, from 1958 onwards, the service was suspended but the route was revitalised in 1964 when the converted car carrier *Falaise* arrived on station (Chapter 9). The economics of the fast ships was such that for each knot over 21 (the conventional speed of a cross-channel ferry at that time) one ton of oil fuel would propel the ship progressively less distance, until at 24 knots it would only go half as far as the 21 knot ship (given similar

La Duchesse de Bretagne (1950), formerly *Brighton*, alongside at Southampton. (author)

machinery). It was no surprise, therefore, when the *Brighton* stood down from duty in 1965 to operate only at peak weekends. This continued through 1966, although she also undertook a number of excursions. She was sold for further service to Jersey Lines in 1967 and renamed *La Duchesse de Bretagne*. Here she was only partially successful as she remained an extremely expensive unit to operate. Nevertheless, for the next two years she maintained a complicated timetable to Jersey, Guernsey, Cherbourg and St Malo from a variety of UK ports. For this she was given a roll-on car carrying capacity (25 cars) with loading flaps onto the Upper Deck. She was sold for demolition in 1970.

Just as the pioneer single reduction geared turbine ferry had been named *Normannia* on completion in 1911, so the first double reduction geared ferry to be commissioned was also given this famous name. The new *Normannia* was the first cross-channel steamer to be equipped with the higher speed Pametrada design turbine units. Together they generated 6,000 kilowatts taking steam at 340°C at a pressure of 24 bar from two Foster Wheeler oil fired boilers. Coupled to twin shafts via double reduction gears she managed a trials speed of nearly 21 knots at 275 revolutions per minute. Her designed speed was 19 knots and, interestingly, she was required to steam backwards at equivalent maximum full power. She was built with Denny-Brown stabilisers.

The *Normannia* was delivered from William Denny early in 1952 and commenced on the British Transport Commission Southern Region Southampton to Le Havre service on 3rd March. She was a three decked ship and her pedigree clearly reflected the earlier *Falaise* (Chapter 9). There was a single hold forward, and accommodation was provided for 780 first class and 630 third class passengers. She maintained the Le Havre service until October 1963. Each year the *Normannia*

Normannia (1952), seen after her conversion to a stern loading car ferry, at Dover in July 1968. (author)

carried out a number of relief duties including standing in at Harwich for the collision damaged *Duke of York* in 1953. During the winter of 1963/64, she was taken in hand at Palmer's Hebburn yard for conversion to a stern loading car carrier for the Dover to Boulogne service. She was given space for 110 cars at the expense of the lower saloon and her passenger certificate was reduced to 500. At the same time, the Bridge Deck was extended right to the stern, and the forward saloon was completely redesigned. This work reduced her gross tonnage from 3,543 to 2,217.

On 9th July 1974 the *Normannia* was holed against obsolete stone work on the Admiralty Pier at Dover. She was towed rapidly into the Tidal Basin where she was able to lie on the bottom in shallow water on an even keel with flooding in the main turbine room and tunnel spaces. She was later towed to Middlesbrough for repairs and resumed a somewhat nomadic life on the South Coast, being temporarily reregistered in Calais under SNCF ownership during the 1973 season. She was given a bow thrust unit in 1975 to help with work on the Channel Islands routes, finishing in the summer of 1977 on a single daily round trip from Dover to Boulogne, with limited service between Newhaven and Dieppe and on the Channel Islands routes the following year. She left in November 1978 for the breakers after a prospective sale to Middle Eastern interests fell through.

The *Normannia* had been launched on 19th July 1951. On 14th December she was followed into the Clyde at Dumbarton by the purpose built car ferry *Lord Warden*. This was the first turbine car ferry to be built, but she was preceded by the two motor ships named *Princess Victoria* which had been built in 1939 and 1946, both as stern loading car ferries. The former was lost in the war but the latter foundered with great loss of life in 1953, shortly after the *Lord Warden* had entered service; this tragedy delayed any further stern loading car ferries being built by the British Transport Commission for a number of years.

The *Lord Warden* had the same machinery arrangement as the *Normannia*, save for Babcock & Wilcox boilers rather than Foster Wheeler. The

Lord Warden (1952), reversing up to her berth at the Eastern Docks in Dover. (author)

Lord Warden maintained the same service speed of 20 knots but could only manage 16 knots astern. On trials she maintained a speed of over 21 knots at 267 revolutions per minute. She was built with a bow thruster and with stabilisers. Her gross tonnage was 3,333 and she was 106 m long by 18 m broad (length to breadth ratio of 6.0). Her stern doors were electrically driven, and were built to the same design as the half doors of the train ferries. She could accommodate 120 cars on one deck, and 986 passengers, with twin berths for 14 of them. The passenger accommodation on B Deck above the car deck comprised a lounge, tea bar forward, restaurant aft, a gift shop, bureau de change, AA/RAC office, passport office and purser's office. There was a smoke room bar forward on A Deck (the Promenade Deck).

The maiden voyage of the *Lord Warden* was from Dover to Boulogne on 16th June 1952. During her first year in service cars were craned aboard although roll-on facilities were already available at Berth 13 in Boulogne. In 1956 her funnel was adapted to mitigate the down draft of oil fumes, and in 1964 she became the guinea pig for the new Sealink colours of blue hull and red funnel, later with the British Rail twin arrow device added in white. She also acquired pale green upperworks before it was realised that this had a camouflage effect at sea and so the superstructure again reverted to white.

In 1970 the *Lord Warden* transferred to Dover-Calais work and she maintained the Golden Arrow passenger service for three weeks in February 1972. In the 1970s she became spare ship at Dover and was seen also at Weymouth, Newhaven and Folkestone and at Fishguard and Holyhead. At this stage in her career her inability to carry more than one heavy goods vehicle seriously limited her viability. Nevertheless, in 1978 her hinged half gates were replaced with hydraulically operated gates that gave protection up to B Deck level, although this work now prevented her from carrying even one high sided vehicle. The following year, however, she undertook her final sailing inbound from Dun Laoghaire to Holyhead on 8th September and was then sold for further work in the Red Sea, only to

Manxman (1955) in the Mersey, off the Princes Landing Stage. (Malcolm McRonald)

be broken up two years later.

Following in the lines of the post-war quintet of Isle of Man steamers, a sixth ship, of similar design, was ordered from Cammell Laird in March 1953. The ship, the *Manxman*, was launched at Birkenhead on 8th February 1955. Although similar in many respects to her predecessors, she was equipped with fundamentally more advanced machinery, and was in fact the third cross-channel steamer to be equipped with two Pametrada design engines and double reduction gears. Superheated steam at 24 bar drove the turbine rotors at 4,300 revolutions per minute, but this was reduced, via double reduction gearing, to drive the twin propellers at a speed of only 270 revolutions per minute. This arrangement generated the same power of 6,300 kilowatts as the earlier quins, but did so in a far more efficient and cost effective manner. On her trials, in May 1955, she managed nearly 22 knots over the measured mile. The new ship cost £847,000.

The *Manxman* had a certificate for 2,302 passengers in two classes and required a crew of 68. Outwardly, the main difference from the quins was that she had her boats slung on Welin gravity davits; this gave her a much less cluttered Upper Deck. Her maiden voyage took place from Douglas to Liverpool on 20th May, under the command of Captain P J Bridson, with delegates of the Union of Post Office Workers returning from their annual conference. Once she had settled in to the service she attained a reputation for comfort and reliability. Her efficient propulsion system placed her as the main winter ship, supported by the *King Orry* (Chapter 9). Both ships received extensions to the Bridge Deck in 1960 to provide stowage for additional life rafts.

The *Manxman* ploughed a successful and largely uneventful career on the Irish Sea. There was a minor stranding in the Mersey in September 1957, a minor collision in thick fog inbound in January 1959, and a winters day in 1965 when she was successively struck by the ferry *Royal Daffodil* and, later the same day, by the tug *Cedargarth* whilst lying alongside at Princes Landing Stage. The *Manxman* was displaced to seasonal use in the mid

1960s. She undertook a brief spell deputising on the Burns & Laird Line Ardrossan to Belfast service standing in for the *Irish Coast* which in turn covered the break down of the *Royal Ulsterman* on the Glasgow to Belfast overnight service.

Towards the end of her working life the *Manxman* became the only remaining classic passenger cross-channel ferry, whilst other younger units in the British Rail and Sealink fleets had been sold or converted for roll-on vehicle and passenger duties. At the end of the 1982 season she was placed on the sale list. Her final passenger sailing was a Liverpool day excursion to Douglas on 4th September and she later sailed with about 1,000 passengers on a single trip to Preston on 3rd October to take up a static role for her new owners Marda (Squash) Limited. She has subsequently had a nomadic existence and to date has not found permanent gainful employment in her intended role as a static entertainment centre.

Although the former London, Midland & Scottish Railway night passenger service from Heysham to Belfast had not lost any of its ships in the war, it was nevertheless in need of updated tonnage by the early 1950s. The cheapest tender received for the new buildings was from William Denny, but the yard was unable to provide three ships in the required timescale, and Denny became the lead yard in a contract in which Harland & Wolff built the first two ships. Denny should have supplied all the structural plans to Harland & Wolff but, in the event, Harlands overtook Denny and built their two ships to their own structural design. Consequently, the Denny ship had a stiffener (stringer) at Lower Deck level through the engine and boiler rooms whereas the two Harland ships had stronger frames. Although all three ships were mainly riveted, the deck plating on the Denny ship was to a clinker construction whereas the others were flush. All three were divided into eleven watertight compartments.

The *Duke of Lancaster* was launched by Harland & Wolff on 14 December 1955, and the *Duke of Argyll* followed on 12th January 1956. Denny

Duke of Lancaster (1956), as built, arriving stern first at Heysham, in the summer of 1967. (author)

Seen leaving Heysham, the *Duke of Argyll* (1956) after her conversion to a stern loading car ferry. (author)

Duke of Rothesay (1956), as a side loading car ferry, coming alongside at Fishguard during 1969. (author)

launched the *Duke of Rothesay* on 10th February 1956. They each had the now conventional twin Pametrada design turbine units with double reduction gears and twin screws. They were the first ships to be given thin walled bearings, and these at first caused vibration problems as discovered during the trials of the *Duke of Lancaster.* Steam was supplied at 30 bar from two Babcock & Wilcox boilers. Astern power for the long journey in reverse up Belfast Lough was 60% of forward. Although capable of 21 knots, the ships were generally steamed at between 14 and 19 knots on the overnight service, which included a Sunday night service, summer only. However, in later years, summer daylight services were introduced and full power was then required.

In sympathy with international politics of the 1950s, the three ships were equipped with an external spray system which was designed to wash down the superstructure and decks in the event of nuclear fall-out. This system was later copied on the *Hebrides* and her two sisters, which were built in the 1960s by the Scottish Office for David MacBrayne.

The three Dukes had two holds, one forward and one aft and could carry crane loaded cars, and, of course, cattle. Passenger accommodation was in two classes: 600 first class with berths for 240, and 1,200 second class with berths for 214. Accommodation was on three decks and widespread use of plastic veneers gave the ships a modern and light appearance. First class was on the Boat Deck and Promenade Deck with an observation lounge forward, and the Dining Saloon was on the Upper Deck below. The second class lounges and cafeteria were on the Upper Deck with further accommodation on the Lower Deck. The officers' accommodation was placed before the funnel on the Bridge Deck.

The ships were delivered between August and December 1956 and their arrival allowed the 1928-built sisters of the same names (Chapter 4) to be retired. The new ships had a number of innovative features: Mather & Platt multi-spray fire protection equipment, aluminium lifeboats, the now standard stabilisers and bow rudders, and modern navigational aids such as echo sounding radio direction finding and, of course, radar.

Of the three, the *Duke of Lancaster* was used seasonally for cruises to Scotland and near Continental destinations. For this, her passenger accommodation was one-class and all cabins had direct access to bathrooms.

The trio continued at Heysham for the next eleven years, after which the *Duke of Rothesay* was converted by Cammell Laird for service out of Fishguard, where she commenced in early 1967 as a side loading car carrier. The Main Deck was completely remodelled to accommodate 110 cars through side doors, and the passenger complement was reduced to 1,400 in one-class. She survived on this route until 1975 when she was sold for demolition at Faslane. Just as the old *Duke of Lancaster* (Chapter 4) had been haunted, so the younger *Duke of Rothesay* occasionally frightened her crew. The night watchmen always worked in pairs when the ship was overnight on the Lay-By Berth at Heysham in case desk drawers should open or paint tins rattle!

The other two sisters, the *Duke of Lancaster* and *Duke of Argyll*, remained at Heysham in the late 1960s amid mounting rumours that the Heysham-Belfast service would be closed. In the event, they were both converted to stern loading car ferries in the winter of 1969/70 by their builder, Harland & Wolff. In this capacity they could carry 105 cars, although the headroom to the car deck was a mere 2 m, and 1,200 one-class passengers with cabin accommodation for 400 of them. This was accomplished by building out over the after well deck to provide a new lounge and seating accommodation. A summer only, daylight service to Belfast commenced with the return of the converted ferries to Heysham.

The new car ferry service was successful, but it lost heavily to the inauguration of the Cairnryan to Larne passenger route introduced by Townsend Thoresen in July 1974. It was inevitable that closure would follow unless the service could be revitalised with new ships. The end took place on 5th April 1975, the *Duke of Lancaster* inbound to Heysham and the *Duke of Argyll* out to Belfast. The service had been started by the Midland Railway in 1904 and the last three ships on the route were built very much in the style of their predecessors; the 1956 Dukes were definitely the last of the traditional Irish Sea cross channel steamers. The *Duke of Lancaster* is retained as a hulk near Mostyn in North Wales whereas the *Duke of Argyll* was gutted by fire at Hong Kong in 1995, under the name *Zenith*, and later broken up. The passenger service remained unavailable until it was reopened in 1999 by the high speed *Seacat Danmark*.

The Motor Ship

The development of the marine internal combustion engine and the increasing efficiency and cost effectiveness of that engine inevitably drove the steam turbine ships to the breakers. The very first large motor driven cross-channel ferries were the Belfast Steamship Company's trio *Ulster Monarch, Ulster Queen* and *Ulster Prince* which entered service in 1929 and 1930. They were powered by twin 10 cylinder Harland B & W oil engines which sustained a service speed of 18 knots for the overnight Liverpool to Belfast service on which they had berths for 401 first class and could carry 493 third class passengers. Mockingly the new motor ships had two funnels, the forward one being a dummy. Proof that the diesel engine could also maintain fast cross-channel services came in 1934 when the Belgian Government commissioned the motor ship *Prince Baudouin* to add to its fleet of 10 fast steam turbine ships. The *Prince Baudouin* had twin sets of 12 cylinder two stroke Sulzer Diesels and managed over 25 knots on trials to become the fastest motor ship afloat. The Belgian Government commissioned no further turbine ships.

The Dutch built their first motor ships in 1939 with the commissioning of the 23 knot pair *Koningin Emma* and *Prinses Beatrix*. However, the Zeeland Steamship Company, who never operated turbine ships, built the steam reciprocating engined *Prinses Juliana* and the *Mecklenburg* as late as 1920 and 1922 respectively. These were copies of a pair built by Fairfields for the company in 1909 also with steam reciprocating engines but capable of maintaining a speed of 23 knots. The 1920s pair were built in Flushing as Fairfields were unable to guarantee delivery, hence the use of steam reciprocating engines rather than turbines at this late stage. The progression from steam piston engines to fast diesels was logical for their next order in view of the earlier success of the Belgian *Prince Baudouin*.

The first British railway owned cross-channel motor ships were the *Princess Victoria* of 1939 and her almost identical namesake of 1946. These were followed by the *Cambria* and *Hibernia* in 1948, although there were no further diesels until 1967 when the *Antrim Princess* was completed for the Stranraer to Larne route. Needless to say, the Coast Lines Seaway continued to build only motorships following the delivery of the *Ulster Monarch* and her sisters.

THE CAR FERRIES

Maid of Kent (1959), affectionately known at Dover as the 'pocket liner'. (author)

The Dover train ferries (Chapter 8) were the first stern loading steam turbine ferries, and the Dover car ferry *Lord Warden* (Chapter 10) was the first dedicated car ferry with steam turbine propulsion. The loss of the motor driven car ferry *Princess Victoria* in the North Channel in 1953 set back the building of further stern loaders for the railways until the late 1950s when the *Maid of Kent* was commissioned for the service between Dover and Boulogne. From that time on, all the steam turbine car ferries were equipped with Pametrada design turbines and double reduction gearing.

The *Maid of Kent* was built by William Denny and launched on 27th November 1958. She had a gross tonnage of 4,413 (later reduced to 3,920) and was 106 m long by 18 m broad (length to breadth ratio of 5.9). Two Babcock & Wilcox boilers supplied steam at a pressure of 24 bar and temperature of 340°C. On trials the new ship achieved 21 knots at 268 revolutions per minute.

She was a most attractive looking vessel and was quickly dubbed 'the pocket liner'. Accommodation for passengers included a restaurant, lounge and buffet as well as passenger cabins on the Main Deck, with a smoke room on the Upper Deck. The main Vehicle Deck was accessed through hydraulically raised stern doors, and there were ramps to single lane Mezzanine Decks on the outside and at the forward part of the ship, with inner lanes aft retaining the full headroom of 3.5 m. The exhaust vents from the boilers split the middle part of the car deck into two. Innovations, other than a completely enclosed car deck, included a Voith Schneider bow thrust unit of about 4 tons thrust.

With a capacity for 190 cars and 1,000 one-class passengers, the ship was an immediate success with the travelling public. Her monopoly on the Dover Strait as the newest and most up-to-date car ferry was short lived as Townsend Brothers introduced the even more forward looking motor driven car ferry *Free Enterprise* (later *Free Enterprise I*) to the Dover station in 1962. Nevertheless, the *Maid of Kent* proved a popular unit throughout her career, although her limited capacity for long wheel-based and high sided vehicles became an encumbrance in her later years.

Life was not altogether incident free for the *Maid of Kent* : for example, she damaged her stern at Dover at the height of the summer season in 1970, and collided with the quay at Boulogne in September 1973. After the latter incident she was prepared for the new Weymouth to Cherbourg route which she commenced on 6th April 1974, although engine problems put her out of service for much of April and all of May.

The *Maid of Kent* spent a short period operating out of Fishguard in 1976 although she stayed principally on the seasonal Cherbourg link from Weymouth. For the 1979 season she received considerable improvements to her passenger accommodation, but it was recognised that her inability to carry other than cars and a few smaller freight vehicles and coaches was a major drawback. Her last season was 1981, and her final scheduled inbound service was on 2nd October under the command of Captain Hurd-Wood. However, damage to the Channel Islands motor ship *Earl William* allowed her to continue on the Weymouth to Jersey and Guernsey service until the end of October. She was then sold for demolition in Spain following a short period of lay up at Newhaven.

The loss of the *Princess Victoria* in 1953 had left the Stranraer to Larne service desperately in need of roll-on roll-off tonnage. Although the *Hampton Ferry* and *Shepperton Ferry* had been periodically drafted in, the popularity of the service was declining. Worse still, rumours of rail closures in the Stranraer area were circulating, when in 1957 an announcement was made that a new passenger and car carrying ship would be provided. The new ship was eventually launched from the yard of William Denny on 5th April 1961 and given the new style name *Caledonian Princess.* Not only did she set the pattern for new nomenclature on the route, but she also sported two red lions 'rampant' on her yellow and black top funnels, the colours of the newly formed Caledonian Steam Packet Company (Irish Services) Limited.

The *Caledonian Princess* was equipped with twin turbines and two Babcock & Wilcox boilers which generated steam at 27 bar. This arrangement gave her a comfortable service speed of 20 knots, and astern power amounted to 85% of forward. She was an extremely manoeuvrable ship with twin rudders, bow thrust unit and bow rudder. She was the first railway ship to be fitted with Denny Brown AEG folding stabilisers. Because of caution over criticism on the grounds of safety, the stern door was designed to swing outwards and upwards so that any mechanical failure would lock it shut and make it watertight.

As built, the *Caledonian Princess* could carry 400 first class and 1,000 second class, and had berths for 82 first and 94 second class passengers. She could also accommodate 104 cars or 50 cars and about 30 larger vehicles, and there were also stalls for up to 70 head of cattle. The Car Deck attained the full height aft only, as forward of the funnel casing the Lower Deck contained also the cafeteria and dining saloon. On the Main Deck were the lounge bar and smoke room with another

Caledonian Princess (1961) off the Holyhead breakwater in September 1974. (author)

lounge on the Upper Deck. The second class lounge carried two 8 m long black and white murals in plastic Wareite. The theme was Celtic life, including Celtic crosses, standing stones, coracles, cottages, donkeys and a boy staring out to sea. The maiden voyage of the *Caledonian Princess* took place on 16th December 1961; there was immediate talk of a sister ship but none was forthcoming.

In her first year of operation, with two round trips per day (one on Sundays), the *Caledonian Princess* encouraged a 20% increase in passenger traffic and a 35% increase in vehicles. Within three years of her entering service it was necessary to bring the new cargo and cattle carrier *Slieve Donard* up from Holyhead to help take an additional 60 cars at a time on the summer services, and by 1965 it was recognised that further dedicated tonnage would be necessary. By 1969 the *Caledonian Princess* was temporarily displaced to the Fishguard route for which side doors were cut into the hull to provide access to the car deck. After a temporary return to the North Channel she became a nomad, with service on many of the south coast routes. Her final service took place between Dover and Boulogne on 26th September 1969 after which the ship was withdrawn and later sold for static use at a variety of UK locations.

Only two further car ferries equipped with steam turbine engines (the *Dover* and *Holyhead Ferry I*) were built for the railways. All subsequent units were motor ships. Before these last two steamers were designed, however, the Isle of Man Steam Packet Company also built and commissioned two further steam turbine engined ships. Broadly similar to the *Manxman* of 1955 (Chapter 10) the quasi-sisters *Manx Maid* and *Ben-my-Chree* had updated accommodation and improved boilers (Babcock & Wilcox integral furnace boilers rather than the sectional header type), but are perhaps best remembered for their innovative spiral loading roadway to the Car Deck. This was in response to the need to load and unload at a variety of ports, none of which at that time had stern loading linkspan facilities. The spiral roadway made five turns, three aft and two forward through the Main Deck up to the Promenade Deck, and was

The unimaginatively named *Holyhead Ferry I* (1965), approaching Dover stern first in September 1973. (author)

Manx Maid (1962) seen in the Mersey, summer 1969. Note the side ports to the spiral loading roadway aft. (author)

a means of allowing access to the quayside through side loading doors at five different levels, irrespective of the height of the quay or the state of the tide; there is a 7 m tidal range at Douglas. The drawback of the system was that only cars and light vans could be accommodated, and the spiral roadway created largely dead space with stowage for motor cycles and occasionally also cars. A turntable was fitted at the forward end of the car deck.

As the first Isle of Man ship designed as a roll-on car carrier the *Manx Maid* was also innovative for the company as the first to be built with stabilisers. She was the thirteenth Isle of Man boat to be built by Cammell Laird (the cost was £1,087,000) and she was launched into the Mersey on 23rd January 1962. Her length was 99 m and breadth 15 m giving her a length to breadth ratio of 6.3. She was designed with two pole masts, a raked stem and a cruiser stern and was equipped with electric hydraulic steering gear, a single main rudder and a bow rudder. The watertight bulkheads were fitted with sliding doors which could be opened and shut from the bridge. The twin turbine units comprised ahead impulse type units and an impulse astern turbine incorporated in the ahead casings; the astern turbines provide 65% of the total forward power of 7,000 kilowatt. A speed of 21 knots was achieved with a propeller speed of 285 revolutions per minute.

The *Manx Maid* had four passenger decks. The fore ends and sides of the Promenade and Shelter Decks were enclosed in screens and there were large windows along the Promenade Deck public rooms. The main lounge was situated at the forward end of the Promenade Deck, and featured settees, tub chairs and small tables. First class passengers also had access to general and ladies' saloons on the Lower Deck, and a dining saloon and a smoke room on the Promenade Deck. Second class passengers were provided with a general saloon, lounge, ladies' room and smoking room, along with a buffet and bar. There was even a fish and chip bar, and there were also eight private cabins. In all, a total passenger complement of 1,400 was catered for by a crew of 60, and there was garage space for up to 70 light vehicles.

The maiden voyage of the new car ferry took place out of Liverpool on 23rd May 1962 under the command of Captain Edward Quirk, who had been the Chief Officer aboard the when she was lost at Dunkerque (Chapter 7). The new car ferry was an immediate success and took her place on the subsequent winter service alongside the *Manxman* (see Chapter 10). During her career, the *Manx Maid* suffered occasionally from steering defects, once towed in stern first up the Mersey on 22nd July 1967 and later, following similar failure, recovered from the Queens Channel by tugs in February 1968. In the meantime a sister had been built (at a cost of £1,400,000) and delivered by Cammell Laird (the last ship they were to build for the Manx company); launched on 10th December 1965, the second turbine driven car ferry was given the name *Ben-my-Chree*. She too was under the command of Captain Quirk for her maiden voyage which took place on 12th May 1966. Four days later, she and her sister were laid up at Barrow until early July during the national seamen's strike; however, on Sunday 15th May she did manage to operate a sell-out inaugural round the island cruise.

Although the new steamers were no match for some of their really fast predecessors, the new *Ben-my Chree* attained the fastest recorded Ardrossan-Douglas run in September 1966 with a time of 4 hours and 50 minutes. Both ships were converted to single-class in time for the 1967 season, and both received steam powered bow thrust units in 1979. By then two motor ships had entered the fleet, designed broadly around the same spiral loading concept - but the fuel economy of these newer ships ultimately placed the future of the steamers in doubt. The price of oil fuel had increased dramatically from 1974 onwards, and the company's annual fuel bill had increased from only £200,000 per year in 1973, to £1,270,000 in 1978. The last of the classic steamers, the *Manxman*, was retired in 1982 following two loss making years for the Isle of Man Steam Packet Company.

Competition from the Manx Line at Heysham (the companies eventually merged in 1985), a decline in tourist numbers, and in 1984 a further increase of 34% in the price of heavy grade fuel oil

Ben-my-Chree (1966) in the Mersey, bound for Douglas, in July 1969. (author)

inevitably hastened the end of the two steam turbine car ferries. The *Manx Maid* finished on 9th September 1984 and the *Ben-my-Chree* on 17th September; both ships were placed on the sale list and laid-up at Birkenhead. In the event, both were sold early the following year, but the *Ben-my-Chree* was chartered back from her new American owners and temporarily registered in Liverpool to run relief sailings out of Heysham for the three week TT race period at the end of May the following year. The *Manx Maid* was eventually demolished in 1986 after attempts at static use in Bristol had failed, and the *Ben-my-Chree*, her American project having fallen through, also went to the breakers, finally being towed from Birkenhead in August 1989. This was very much the end of an era, and it should be remembered that only five years later high speed catamaran services were to commence running to the island.

Two final turbine-driven car ferries were also built for British Rail. These ships carried the inspired names of *Dover*, the result of a schools competition to find the most original name for a new Dover to Calais stern loader, and *Holyhead Ferry I*, the innovative choice of name for the first car ferry to serve Holyhead! Nevertheless, they were distinguished ships for three reasons: they were the last turbine cross-channel ferries to be built (along with the *Ben-my-Chree*), their boilers generated steam at a higher pressure than any other cross-channel ship, and they were later converted from stern loading only to become the only drive through steam turbine ferries.

The first of the two ships to be commissioned was the *Holyhead Ferry I*. She was a product of Hawthorn Leslie at Newcastle and had a gross tonnage of some 3,879. She was equipped with the now conventional Pametrada turbines which gave her a service speed of 21 knots. She also had twin rudders, a bow thrust unit and, of course, stabilisers. The Car Deck could accommodate 125 cars, 25 of them on the Mezzanine Deck which was accessed via hydraulic ramps. There were two turntables forward, and the stern door, which was 6 m wide, was operated by a Kone hydraulic hinge, a unique feature in the railway fleet. There were also

Dover (1965) in the Dover Strait in July 1973. She was the last turbine steamer built for the railways. (author)

two hatches placed forward, of which only one was normally used in service. These were designed with the dual purpose of providing crane access to the car deck in case the stern doors failed, as well as allowing crane loaded mail and baggage access to the car deck forward.

The passenger accommodation of the *Holyhead Ferry I* included a large lounge and a lounge tea bar, plus a restaurant and smoke room on the Main Deck, and there were a number of private cabins on the Boat Deck. The new ship entered service in July 1965 under Captain Richard Roberts, displacing the elderly *Princess Maud* from the Holyhead to Dun Laoghaire route (Chapter 8). She maintained two round trips per day, leaving Holyhead at 10.45 and 20.15 hours and Dun Laoghaire at 06.00 and 15.30 hours. The *Holyhead Ferry I* very quickly proved the demand for the new service and was soon running to capacity.

Although there had been an option for a second vessel, the need for such an order arose suddenly when an extra berthing slot was made available at Dover Eastern Docks and the order had to be placed instead with Swan Hunter & Wigham Richardson. This was the *Dover*, which entered service on the Calais service on 6th June 1965 resplendent in the new blue hull colours and red and black funnel of British Rail. To all intents and purposes, the two ships were sisters, but there were a number of minor differences, not least a duty free shop and the removal of the galley aft on board the *Dover*. In addition, the Mezzanine Deck was enlarged to accommodate 40 cars.

The *Dover* was displaced from her home port in 1969 and went then to join the *Holyhead Ferry I* at Holyhead for a summer season starting 22nd May. The following day, fire in the railway bridge over the Menai Strait severed the railway link and the passenger service was temporarily transferred to Heysham. The car ferries remained in service out of Holyhead and also included three scheduled trips per week from Dun Laoghaire to Heysham. The latter service continued through the next summer but was terminated in September 1971. The two ships were thereafter used on a variety of services in addition to the central Irish Sea route.

In 1976 the *Holyhead Ferry I* was sent to Swan Hunter for major alterations to increase her freight vehicle capacity and allow bow loading. The cost of this work was some £1,850,000. She emerged with additional lifeboats, although with a greatly reduced passenger certificate of 725, but with increased car capacity of 205, and with the new name of *Earl Leofric.* On 23rd September 1976 she took up station at Dover. The *Dover* was dealt with similarly although with less of an emphasis on freight traffic. She was sent to Aalborg Werft and was converted for drive through work under the new name of *Earl Siward* at a cost of £1,960,000. She returned to service on 1st July 1977 and was employed mainly in the Irish Sea, although both ships worked the Dover to Calais service throughout 1979. The *Earl Leofric* was withdrawn in 1980 and sold for demolition early the following year. The *Earl Siward* survived until 1982 when she was sold for further service in the Mediterranean, later returning to the UK in a static role. Unhappily, all the spares for the two ships had been dispatched to the breakers yard with the *Earl Leofric,* leaving her half-sister rather vulnerable; it was not surprising, therefore, that she was reduced to a static role only five years later.

AVALON - MYTHICAL IDEAL

The ultimate commercial application of the steam turbine was the magnificent American liner *United States*. She had been built in 1952 and on her first transatlantic voyage broke the previous best record of the *Queen Mary* by nearly 4 knots. On trials, she achieved a staggering 43 knots; details of her engines remained classified as a military secret throughout her 17 year career on the New York to Southampton run. She has two nearly identical engine rooms providing 160,000 kilowatts. The forward engine room propelled the outboard screws, the aft engine room the inboard pair of propellers.

That being so, the demands on the British cross-channel steamers in the 1950s and 1960s were somewhat more modest - a design speed of 21 knots having become standard on many daylight services in post-war years. The most powerful British cross-channel steamer at that time was the *Brighton* which generated 14,000 kilowatts (Chapter 10). However, economics finally came to a head during the winter of 1973/74, when crisis in the Middle East forced the price of heavy fuel oil up from around £8 per ton to about £34 per ton in the space of four months. Most operators were forced to add oil surcharges to their published fares, and those with an inefficient vessel on their hands had to look very carefully at the future.

Before the constraints of fuel efficiency and the increased cost effectiveness of the internal combustion engine finally took their toll, four notable classic steam turbine vessels were yet to enter the nationalised railway fleet.

The first was a conventional passenger ferry built by the French, which entered the British registry for only a brief period in the 1950s and early 1960s. This ship had been built and equipped very much to the old design with single reduction gears, albeit with triple reduction turbines which generated a power of 16,000 kilowatts. This was the *Londres*, ordered as one of a pair in 1939 and built at Le Havre by Forges et Chantiers de la Méditerranée in time for the invading Germans to fit her out in 1940 as the mine layer *Lothringen*. At the end of hostilities she was found lying at Kiel in a poor state of repair, but was reconditioned and finally entered commercial service between Newhaven and Dieppe under the French flag in the spring of 1947. Her sister was only launched in March 1946 and was given the name *Arromanches* in honour of the Allied landing there in 1944.

Both ships flew the French flag and were manned by French crews. However, in 1953 the new French single reduction geared steamer *Lisieux* was delivered for the Newhaven to Dieppe service also from the same Le Havre yard, and she displaced the elderly *Worthing* (Chapter 4). In order to maintain the balance of two British and two French ferries, the *Londres* was transferred to the British flag in time for the 1955 season. Described as singularly unattractive, she was nevertheless a very powerful unit capable of maintaining the long crossing at 24 knots. The passenger accommodation was laid out on two decks and she could carry 1,450 passengers.

The *Londres* was finally displaced in 1963 in anticipation of the newly converted car carrier *Falaise* which started on the route the following summer (Chapter 9). On 1st January 1964, the *Londres* was towed from lay up at Southampton to Piraeus, where she was refitted and re-engined as the Typaldos Brothers motor cruise ferry *Ionian II*. Later bankruptcy of her new owners coincided with the ship being gutted by fire in 1966, beached at

Piraeus and broken up.

Next a pair of passenger ships were built by J Samuel White at Cowes for service between Weymouth and the Channel Isles. These were the *Caesarea* and *Sarnia*, whose dimensions provided optimum use of the constraints of St Helier and St Peter Port harbours. Their draft was a mere 4 m, whilst their gross tonnage was initially measured as 4,174 (later reduced to 3,992), they were only 92 m long and their length to breadth ratio was a stubby 5.6. Although fitted with stabilisers, these ships were no place to be on a winter's evening on the Western Channel! They had the now conventional Pametrada design turbines and double reduction gears which were manufactured by Whites. Steam was supplied at 27 bar at a temperature of 340°C at the superheated outlet. The design service speed of the ships was 19 knots. Equipment included White/Gilljet bow thrusters and a bow rudder with rotary steering gears.

The *Caesarea* was launched at Cowes on 29th January 1960, and her sister the *Sarnia* followed her into the water on 6th September. The two ships represented an investment of £3 million. One-class accommodation for 1,400 included 25 double cabins and two de luxe suites, 12 single cabins, and 44 curtained Pullman type sleeping berths, each with recessed dressing table and easy chair. Much use was made of melamine panelling which gave the ships an air of lightness and space. However, a night aboard these ships, with a full complement of passengers, was indeed a crowded and claustrophobic experience. A single hold was situated forward for the carriage of the mail and baggage – these were truly the last pair of classic cross-channel steamers.

The single-berth cabins were situated on the Promenade Deck along with a smoke room and bar, lounge and buffet. On the Upper Deck were the lounge/buffet, shop and restaurant, and another lounge, cafeteria/bar and ladies' and men's lounges were situated on the Lower Deck. The Promenade Deck bar seated 95 in armchairs and fixed seats with arm rests, and the lounge was panelled in Lebanon cedar with upholstered seating for 142, and a further 117 seats in the bar/buffet. The Upper Deck lounge could seat 136 and the restaurant catered for up to 110 at a single sitting with a further 132 seats in the buffet. Much use was made of cedar panelling, rose wood railings and teak woodwork.

On the Main Deck were port and starboard lounges, each seating 59, complete with overhead luggage racks. Folding doors concealed the embarkation doors. The Main Deck cafeteria/bar had seats for a further 142 and there was a central stairway aft down to the Lower Deck lounges. All the public rooms and the cabin accommodation were heated by steam generated in eight domestic heating boilers to maintain an internal temperature of 19°C as well as the appropriate number of air changes.

There were some initial teething problems with the machinery. The *Caesarea* experienced the same tail vibration problems which earlier ships, notably the *Duke of Lancaster* (Chapter 10), had experienced. This was traced to the bossing supports on the propeller shafts and was rectified by the provision of additional supporting struts. The *Caesarea* carried out her maiden voyage on 2nd December 1960, the *Sarnia* on 13th June 1961. The pair quickly entered the daily routine, earning themselves a reputation for good service and timekeeping. They remained together on the Channel Isles route until the end of the 1975 season when the *Caesarea* was displaced to Dover. The *Sarnia* was by then having recurring problems with her turbines and was out of action for three weeks in the early summer.

Notwithstanding, the *Sarnia* remained at Weymouth until her last sailing from the islands on 4th September 1977. There was one final charter to Guernsey on 10th September and then she was laid up at Weymouth pending sale. In May the following year she was sold to Channel Cruises Limited and renamed *Aquamart* for use in a controversial duty free shopping role working out of Dunkerque and Ostend. Only a few sailings took place before protests from Ostend shopkeepers brought the service to a halt. She did, however, see further service in the Middle East, refitted for stern vehicle loading as the *Golden Star*, later the *Saudi*

A crowded *Caesarea* (1960), seen leaving Weymouth in June 1969. (author)

An equally crowded *Sarnia* (1960), seen off Weymouth during August 1973. (author)

Golden Star, and was eventually disposed of to the breakers in 1987.

The *Caesarea* continued at Dover and Folkestone, albeit with prolonged winter lay ups, finishing on the Dover to Calais service on 27th September 1980. A final excursion under charter to the Dover Rotary Club took place on 4th October before the ship sailed to Hong Kong to become a gambling centre. This venture fell through and the old ship changed owners a number of times before arriving in South Korea in 1986 where she was demolished.

The very last classic turbine steamer of all, some would say the most beautiful, others the best appointed, but certainly the largest, was the Harwich to Hook steamer *Avalon*. The name was originally given to one of the earliest Great Eastern Railway steamers in 1865 and reflects both the Land of Apples where the Celtic Gods were laid to rest as well as the Sixth Century mythical burial ground of King Arthur. Whilst many remember this ship with affection, it should also be remembered that she was designed to a mythical ideal, she was in fact obsolescent before she entered service because only five years later the drive through motor vehicle ferry *St George* arrived on the Hook service.

The *Avalon* was built by Alexander Stephen & Sons at a cost of £2 million. Of all welded construction, she was designed as a three deck ship, and built from prefabricated units each weighing up to 40 tons. The new ship was equipped with two Pametrada design turbine units, articulated locked-train double reduction gears, and with steam generated by two Foster Wheeler boilers at 24 bar at a temperature of 340°C at the superheater outlets. The boilers worked on the open stokehold forced draught system. There were twin rudders aft, operated by AEG rotary vane electric-hydraulic Brown Brothers gears, a bow rudder and a Vickers side-thrust bow unit, and twin four-blade propellers which were 4 m in diameter. Her service speed was over 21 knots. The *Avalon* was the first railway ship to be fitted with a biological sewage treatment

Avalon (1963), as built, approaches Parkeston Quay on 30 August 1974, ready for one of her last trips to the Hook. (author)

plant, and the first cross-channel ship to be fully air conditioned throughout. She was built with a most attractive sheer and fine lines, and the bridge was curved between the ends of the open bridge wings.

Steam for domestic services, oil fuel heating units and air conditioning was supplied by two oil-fired Spanner boilers. Four main 400 kilowatt, and one auxiliary 75 kilowatt diesel generators supplied direct current, and two 50 kva diesel alternators supplied power to alternating current equipment including the fluorescent lighting.

There was accommodation for 750 first and second class passengers and berths for 615 in 277 cabins as well as six de luxe cabins on the Promenade Deck, each with a private bathroom. There was limited space for cargo and craned-on cars in the two forward and one aft holds. The *Avalon* was also designed as a one-class cruise ship for 320 passengers. The Lower Deck contained the crew's accommodation and many of the first class cabins. On the Main Deck were the first and second class cabin accommodation as well as the cargo spaces, and on the Upper Deck were the first class restaurant and the smokeroom and bar, as well as the second class cafeteria and smokeroom/bar. The Promenade Deck was mainly given over to crew accommodation. There were two shops.

The first class restaurant was panelled in teak, whereas grained pine was used in the first class bar, along with brass and stainless steel and black leather upholstery. Elsewhere in the ship, melamine plastic veneer over chipboard was used on most bulkheads and deckheads, as well as on the flat surfaces of furniture.

The *Avalon* was launched on 7th May 1963 following delays caused by a tugmen's strike on the Clyde. The *Avalon* joined the *Arnhem* and *Amsterdam* (see Chapter 9) on the Hook service with a maiden voyage on 25th July 1963; her first cruise took place in April 1964. However, at the tender age of only eleven, this last classic turbine steamer was displaced from her designed service by the second motor car ferry *St Edmund*. The steamer was then taken in hand by Swan Hunter at North Shields, where the Lower Deck accommodation was stripped out to make way for two low level car decks accessed through a new stern door. Additional accommodation was provided aft on the Upper Deck to give her a passenger certificate for 1,200 (although still in two classes) and a capability of carrying 200 cars and eight larger commercial vehicles. The car ferry *Avalon* arrived at Fishguard to take up service to Rosslare on 15th July 1975. The conversion work cost some £1,750,000.

In her new role she worked mainly out of Fishguard but did some work out of Holyhead where she became relief ship for the 1979 and 1980 seasons. In 1980 the *Avalon* suffered serious boiler problems. Her final sailing to Holyhead was on 8th September 1980 before she moved later in the month to lay up at Barrow. In December, she left port on her longest voyage, sailing for the breakers yard in Pakistan. The era of the motor driven vehicle ferry had arrived.

Postscript

At the end of 1980, there remained in service the railway steamers *Maid of Kent* and *Earl Siward*, formerly the *Dover*, and the Isle of Man boats *Manxman, Manx Maid* and *Ben-my-Chree*. The *Maid of Kent* was retired in 1981 and the *Earl Siward* in 1982. The *Manxman* finished in active service in 1982, and her two consorts in 1984; the brief reprieve for the *Ben-my-Chree* in 1985 (Chapter 11) had indeed been the end of the cross-channel steamer. The end had come swiftly: in 1960 there were 50 short sea turbine steamers under the red ensign including five excursion ships, but by 1975 there were only 21, of which 2 were excursion steamers. It was the economics of this last decade that nailed the coffin for the cross-channel marine turbine.

Probably the last steam turbine passenger ferry (albeit with electric drive) ever to be built was the *Rangatira* for the Union Steam Ship Company of New Zealand in 1971. She was a replacement for the 1966 built turbo-electric *Wahine* which foundered at Wellington on 10th April 1968. The *Rangatira* only ran on her designed service for three years before she was deemed no longer economically viable and was laid up. After a long

Manxman (1955) remembered: fog on the Mersey, February 1963. (author)

spell as an accommodation vessel, she did eventually see later service in the Mediterranean.

In looking at the UK short sea fleets it must be remembered that many other nations operated turbine steamers plying on their short sea routes. Duckworth and Langmuir, however, described the pre-eminence of the British cross-channel steamer thus:

> *In proportion to her size this type of ship is a triumph of skill in design, having regard to accommodation, draught and speed, and is a peculiarly British triumph at that, as no other country in the world has had such problems to solve. Belgium, France and Japan have some experience in this direction, but we can pride ourselves on great marine achievements in the high speed craft which have maintained our Continental and Irish services for a century. No small part of this was due to Messrs Denny of Dumbarton, now, unfortunately, no longer building ships.*

Other classes of steam turbine ship, however, continued to be built and steam turbine engines remained the preferred motive system for very large oil tankers and dry cargo ships well into the 1980s. Several large passenger units remained in service with their original turbine engines long after they were economically viable (eg the former Canadian Pacific Empresses) whilst several others (eg the *Queen Elizabeth 2*) were converted to diesel propulsion to prolong their economic life.

The significance of the marine turbine in terms of economic and military progress is hard to comprehend, and the role of Sir Charles Parsons in moulding the history of the Twentieth Century can never properly be realised. The apparently relentless advance of the turbine engine in short sea vessels is illustrated by increases in operational steam pressure, whereas generated power increased less markedly and reflects more the occasional building of faster ships (Figure 4). The key engineering developments were single reduction gearing which allowed faster and more efficient turbine speeds, and later the double reduction gear with even faster turbines coupled with increased boiler technology, most notably the introduction of the water tube boiler and the change over from coal to oil fuel.

One of the most critical stages in turbine development occurred in the 1930s. It was then that the turbocharger was being developed for the internal combustion engine. This work required a greater understanding of the processes of converting gaseous energy to motive power, and was accelerated with the military interest in jet engine technology which required a thorough technical understanding of fan hydraulics. It was these developments which passed the British engineer by and which required the formation of the post-war Pametrada consortium to catch up on the pre-war work of the American and German engineers. The marine turbine remains, nevertheless, a British invention which has played a great part in the development of marine engineering, particularly in the promotion of the cross-channel and long distance passenger trade. The steam turbine remains now as the principal means of commercial land-based electricity generation, and will do so for many years to come.

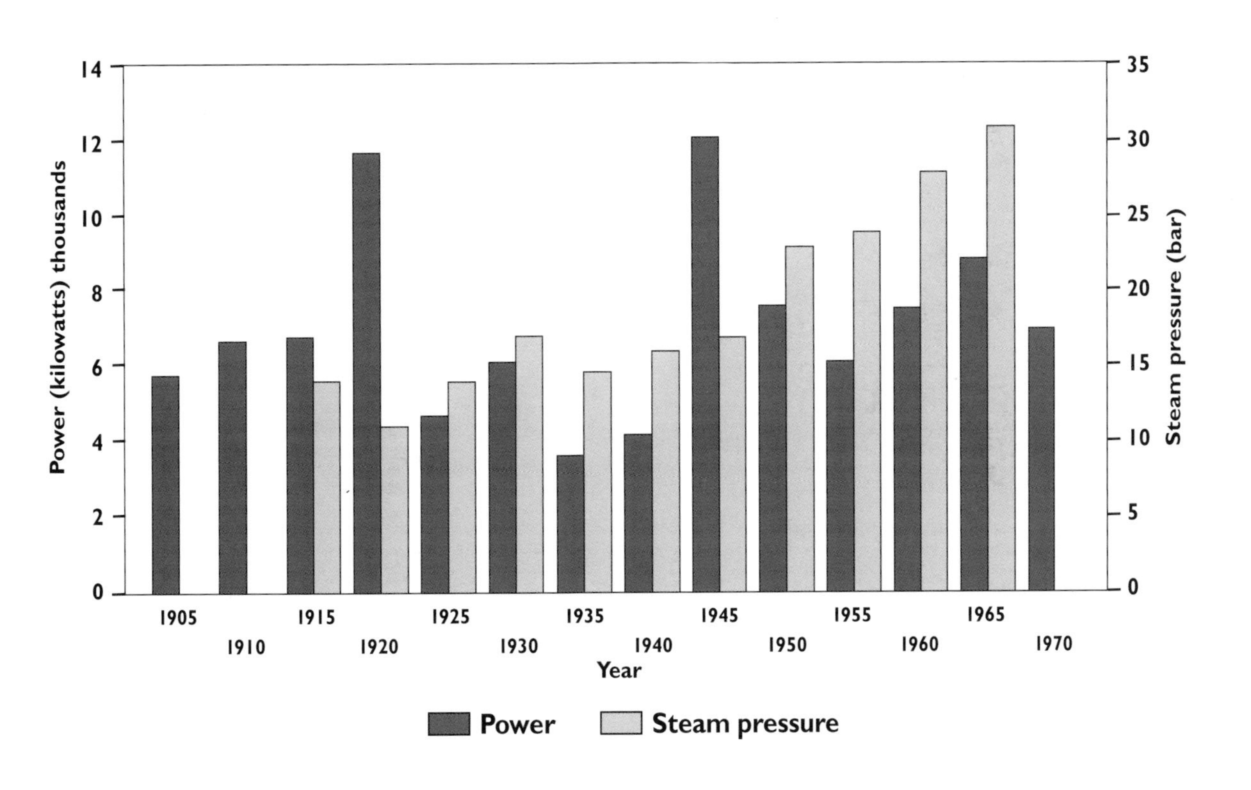

Figure 4.
Average power and steam pressure of steamers built in the five year period prior to the year shown.

Sarnia and Caesarea

These ships were the last pair of passenger-only steam turbine ferries to be built. Their paired single casing impulse type turbines could develop a power of 6,300 kilowatts at 275 propeller revolutions per minute to give a speed of over 19 knots. The astern turbines were housed in the same casings and full astern speed was 15 knots. The twin Foster Wheeler oil-fired boilers were operated on the open stoke-hold system of forced draft, with air supplied from two turbine-driven forced draught fans each supplying $7m^3$ per second to the furnaces and a further $11m^3$ per second to the boilers. The main condensers were Weir regenerative condensers constructed by Whites. Each contained 2,120 aluminium/brass tubes of 6 mm external diameter which provided a massive cooling surface of $370m^2$. Electric current was generated by three 225 kilowatt 220 volt direct current generators.

The *Sarnia* and *Caesarea* each had two continuous decks, the Main and Upper, a Promenade Deck, Boat Deck and Bridge Deck. The hull was constructed on the transverse frame system with riveted strakes and welded butts. There was a cellular bottom between the fore and peak tanks, the latter used for water storage and water ballast. Openings in the eleven transverse watertight bulkheads and the shaft tunnels were fitted with sliding doors which could be operated remotely from the bridge using the ordinary electrical circuit or emergency back-up batteries.

The ships' limited cargo space was situated forward and aft of the accommodation. The hatches on the Upper Deck were of the MacGregor type controlled by Stothert & Pitt worm geared hatch cover winches which were electrically driven. The mooring winches were electrically driven; the capstans were capable of a pull of 7 tons at a rope speed of 0.4 m per second, and there was a windlass forward which had a pull of 16.5 tons at a rope speed of 0.2 m per second. Denny Brown stabilisers were fitted and there was a bow rudder; both bow and main rudders were operated by two German steering gears fitted on the Main Deck.

A high standard of accommodation was provided for the crew of 78. The master had a panelled suite of rooms abaft the wheelhouse on the port side of the chart room. There was cabin accommodation for two deck officers, the pilot, and the radio officer forward on the Boat deck, and the five engineering officers and the electrical officer aft. The petty officers, stewards and remaining crew were accommodated on the Main Deck forward and aft of the passenger accommodation.

The ships carried a Class II Certificate. They had six lifeboats and 45 inflatable rafts. Two of the lifeboats were motor-propelled accident boats, housed below crescent davits behind the bridge. The other boats were hand-powered and mounted on conventional Welin-Machlachlan davits. Navigating equipment included Decca true motion radar and a Decca Navigator. There was a fixed Chernikeef log accessed from the Main Deck and a Kelvin Hughes echo sounder and magnetic compasses, one of which repeated in the wheelhouse and on the bridge wings. The engine room telegraph was electric, and there was a full set of fire and muster alarms, sprinkler alarms, vent trips, and other emergency equipment.

APPENDIX - THE STEAMERS

1) DIRECT DRIVE STEAMERS

Name as built	Dates	Gross tons	Engine power (kW)	Speed (knots)
Turbine Steamers Limited				
King Edward	1901-1952	562		20
Queen Alexandra	1902-1911*			21
Queen Alexandra	1912-1958	785		20
London Brighton & South Coast Railway				
Brighton	1903-1933	1,129	4,400	21
Dieppe	1905-1941	1,210	4,400	21
South Eastern & Chatham Railway				
The Queen	1903-1916	1,676	5,600	21
Invicta	1905-1933	1,680	5,600	21
Onward	1905-1948	1,671	5,600	21
Victoria	1906-1957	1,689	5,600	21
Empress	1907-1933	1,690	5,200	22
Engardine	1911-1941	1,676	6,000	22
Riviera	1911-1957	1,674	6,000	20
Midland Railway				
Manxman	1904-1949	2,086	4,700	22
Londonderry	1904-1936	2,086	4,700	22
Portpatrick & Wigtownshire Joint Railway				
Princess Maud	1904-1932	1,655		20
Princess Victoria	1912-1934	1,678		19
Isle of Man Steam Packet Company				
Viking	1905-1954	1,957	8,200	22
Ben-my-Chree	1908-1917	2,250	10,400	24
Great Central Railway				
Marylebone	1906-1938	1,972		18
Immingham	1906-1915	2,009		18
G&J Burns				
Viper	1906-1948	1,713	5,200	21

Name as built	Dates	Gross tons	Engine power (kW)	Speed (knots)
Fishguard & Rosslare Railway and Harbour Company				
St Patrick	1906-1929	2,531	7,500	20
St David	1906-1933	2,529	7,500	20
St George	1906-1929	2,456	7,500	20
St Andrew	1908-1933	2,528	7,500	20
General Steam Navigation Company				
Kingfisher	1906-1938	982		20
Caledonian Steam Packet Company				
Duchess of Argyll	1906-1970	594		20
Duchess of Montrose	1930-1965	806	3,300	20
Duchess of Hamilton	1932-1974	795	2,800	20
Glasgow & South Western Railway				
Atalanta	1906-1945	486		17
Great Eastern Railway				
Copenhagen	1907-1917	2,570	7,500	20
Munich	1907-1950	2,570	7,500	20
St Petersburg	1910-1941	2,570		20
Lancashire & Yorkshire and London & North Western Railway				
Duke of Argyll	1909-1939	2,052	6,300	19
Duke of Cumberland	1909-1936	2,052	6,300	22
London & South Western Railway				
Caesarea	1910-1950	1,505	4,500	20
Sarnia	1910-1918	1,498	4,500	20
London & North Western Railway				
Greenore	1912-1926	1,488		20
Williamson Buchanan				
Queen Mary	1933	871	2,800	19

*Declared a constructive total loss but rebuilt for further service in Canada.

2) SINGLE REDUCTION GEARED STEAMERS

Name as built	Dates	Gross tons	Engine power (kW)	Speed (knots)
London & South Western Railway				
Hantonia	1911-1952	1,560	3,700	19
Normannia	1911-1940	1,567	3,700	19
Lorina	1918-1940	1,504	3,700	19
Isle of Man Steam Packet Company				
King Orry	1913-1940	1,877	7,000	21
Ben-my-Chree	1927-1965	2,586	7,700	24
Lady of Mann	1930-1971	3,104	8,600	23
Mona's Queen	1934-1940	2,756	6,300	22
Tynwald	1937-1942	2,376	6,300	21
Fenella	1937-1940	2,376	6,300	21
Mona's Queen	1946-1981	2,485	6,300	21
King Orry	1946-1979	2,485	6,300	21
Tynwald	1947-1975	2,493	6,300	21
Snaefell	1948-1978	2,489	6,300	21
Mona's Isle	1951-1980	2,495	6,300	21
London, Brighton & South Coast Railway				
Paris	1913-1940	1,774	10,400	24
South Eastern & Chatham Railway				
Maid of Orleans	1914-1944	2,384	7,500	23
Biarritz	1914-1949	2,495		23
Liverpool & North Wales Steamship Company				
St Seiriol	1914-1918	927		17
St Tudno	1926-1963	2,326	3,000	19
St Seiriol	1931-1962	1,586	2,500	19
London & North Western Railway				
Curraghmore	1919-1935	1,587		20
Cambria	1920-1949	3,445	12,000	24
Anglia	1920-1935	3,460	12,000	24
Scotia	1920-1940	3,441	12,000	24
Hibernia	1920-1949	3,458	12,000	24

Name as built	Dates	Gross tons	Engine power (kW)	Speed (knots)
Great Eastern Railway				
Bruges	1920-1948	2,949		21
Antwerp	1920-1951	2,957		21
Malines	1922-1948	2,969		21
Southern Railway				
St Briac	1924-1942	2,290	3,900	20
Dinard	1924-1970	2,291	3,900	18
Isle of Thanet	1925-1964	2,701	7,000	22
Maid of Kent	1925-1940	2,386	7,000	22
Worthing	1928-1965	2,288	11,000	24
Canterbury	1929-1965	2,912	7,000	23
Isle of Guernsey	1930-1961	2,145	4,000	19
Isle of Jersey	1930-1963	2,143	4,000	19
Brighton	1931-1940	2,391	11,000	25
Isle of Sark	1932-1960	2,211	4,000	19
Brittany	1933-1972	1,445	1,900	14
Shepperton Ferry	1934-1972	2,839	3,300	16
Hampton Ferry	1934-1973	2,839	3,300	16
Twickenham Ferry	1934-1974	2,839	3,300	16
Invicta	1940-1972	4,178	8,200	22
Falaise	1946-1974	3,710	6,300	20
London, Midland & Scottish Railway				
Glen Sannox	1925-1954	664		20
Duke of Rothesay	1928-1956	3,606	6,000	22
Duke of Lancaster	1928-1956	3,608	6,000	20
Duke of Argyll	1928-1956	3,604	6,000	21
Slieve Bloom	1930-1965	1,279	2,100	16
Princess Margaret	1931-1975	2,523	5,600	20
Slieve More	1932-1965	1,397	2,100	17
Princess Maud	1933-1969	2,886	5,600	20
Slieve League	1935-1967	1,342	2,100	17
Duke of York	1935-1975	3,743	6,000	20
Slieve Bearnagh	1936-1972	1,450	2,100	17
Slieve Bawn	1936-1972	1,447	2,100	17
Great Western Railway				
St Julien	1925-1961	1,885	3,200	18
St Helier	1925-1960	1,885	3,200	18

Name as built	Dates	Gross tons	Engine power (kW)	Speed (knots)
Turbine Steamers Limited				
King George V	1926-1981	791	2,600	20
London & North Eastern Railway				
Vienna	1929-1960	4,227	7,500	21
Prague	1930-1947	4,220	7,500	21
Amsterdam	1930-1944	4,220	7,500	21
Arnhem	1947-1969	4,891	9,000	21
Canadian National Railway				
Prince Henry*	1930-1962	5,556		
Fishguard & Rosslare Railway and Harbour Company				
St Patrick	1930-1941	1,911	5,000	22
St Andrew	1932-1967	2,702	5,000	22
St David	1932-1944	2,702	5,000	22
St Patrick	1947-1980	3,482	6,300	20
St David	1947-1980	3,482	6,300	20
Admiralty				
Bittern+	1935-1951			
Halladale	1944-1972	1,370		20
Williamson Buchanan				
Marchioness of Graham	1936-1958	585		18
P&A Campbell				
Empress Queen	1940	1,781		20
French State Railways				
Londres	1940-1966	2,404	16,000	24
British Transport Commission				
Maid of Orleans	1949-1975	3,776	7,500	22
Brighton	1950-1970	2,875	14,000	24
Amsterdam	1950-1981	5,092	9,300	21

*Ministry of War Transport *Empire Parkeston* 1945-1962
+Three Star Shipping *Lady Enchantress* 1946-1950

3) DOUBLE REDUCTION GEARED STEAMERS

Name as built	Dates	Gross tons	Engine power (kW)	Speed (knots)
British Transport Commission				
Normannia	1952-1978	3,543	6,000	19
Lord Warden	1952-1981	3,333	6,000	20
Duke of Lancaster	1956	4,797	7,800	21
Duke of Rothesay	1956-1975	4,780	7,800	21
Duke of Argyll	1956-1995	4,797	7,800	21
Maid of Kent	1959-1982	4,413	8,600	21
Caesarea	1960-1986	4,174	6,700	20
Sarnia	1960-1987	4,174	6,700	20
Avalon	1963-1981	6,584	11,000	21
Isle of Man Steam Packet Company				
Manxman	1955	2,495	6,300	21
Manx Maid	1962-1986	2,724	7,000	21
Ben-my-Chree	1966-1989	2,762	7,000	21
Caledonian Steam Packet Company				
Caledonian Princess	1961	3,630	8,600	20
British Rail				
Dover	1965	3,602	9,000	20
Holyhead Ferry I	1965-1981	3,879	9,000	21

REFERENCES

Periodicals

Paddle Wheels; Sea Breezes.

Books

Anon. 1976. *British Vessels Lost at Sea 1939-45*. Patrick Stephens, Cambridge.

Chappell C 1962. *Island Lifeline*. T Stephenson & Sons, Prescot.

Duckworth C L D and Langmuir G E 1968. *Railway and Other Steamers*. 2nd edition. T Stephenson & Sons, Prescot.

Jane F T 1915. *The British Battle Fleet*. The Library Press Ltd, London

McNeill D B 1969. *Irish Passenger Steamship Services Volume 1*, North of Ireland. David & Charles, Newton Abbot.

McNeill D B 1971. *Irish Passenger Steamship Services Volume 2*, South of Ireland. David & Charles, Newton Abbot.

Robins N S 1995. *The Evolution of the British Ferry*. Ferry Publications, Kilgetty.

Robins N S 1998. *The British Excursion Ship*. Brown, Son & Ferguson, Glasgow.

Thornley F C 1962. *Past and Present Steamers of North Wales*. 2nd edition. T Stephenson & Sons, Prescot.

Wilson R 1991. *Passenger Steamers of the Glasgow & South Western Railway*. Twelveheads Press, Truro.

SHIP NAME INDEX

Names in ordinary typescript are cross-channel turbine steamers. Names in italics are other ferries, passenger liners, cargo ships and ships of the Royal Navy whether turbine driven or not. The prefix HMS is given after the ship name as in *Halladale,* HMS. The year built is given in brackets. Numerals in **bold** indicate where illustrations are located. Numerals in *italics* indicate data in a table.

Other shipping books by Colourpoint:

Passenger Ships of the Irish Sea
Laurence Liddle 1 898392 30 7
£13.99 152pp

In preparation:

Where is she now?
David Latimer
A comprehensive encyclopedia of all world passenger ships of the 20th century, over 3000 tons. Publication in the second half of 2000.

Colourpoint Railway titles:

Title / Author	ISBN	Price
Locomotives of the GNRI		
Norman Johnston	1 898392 48 X	£25.00
The Last Years of 'The Wee Donegal'		
Robert Robotham	1 898392 42 0	£13.99
Isle of Man Classic Steam		
Robert Robotham	1 898392 43 9	£13.99
Fermanagh's Railways – A photographic tribute		
Friel & Johnston	1 898392 39 0	£11.99
The Castlederg and Victoria Bridge Tramway		
E M Patterson	1 898392 29 3	£9.99
Irish Metro-Vick Diesels		
Barry Carse	1 898392 15 3	£4.99
The Warrenpoint Branch		
J D Fitzgerald	1 898392 14 5	£4.99